MAKING CARS AT
LONGBRIDGE

Acknowledgements

The authors would like to thank all who assisted in the preparation of this book, which was originally researched and written in 2005 and extensively revised in 2015. In particular, Archbishop Sentamu for the grant of study leave in 2005 and all at Longbridge Parish Church for their support and patience; the former workforce at MG Rover (in administration) for their co-operation with our photographic survey; the Longbridge photographers, particularly John Chasemore, for painstakingly documenting the factory through 100 years; Mike Murray and St Modwen Properties, PricewaterhouseCoopers, and Nanjing Automobile Corporation for assistance in saving historic material; Lisa Stevens for her expert scanning; John Baker (www.austinmemories.com) for his advice; Claire Farrell of the Longbridge Public Art Project for her support; Amy Rigg at The History Press for her encouragement.

Picture credits

British Motor Industry Heritage Trust (Longbridge and Cowley Photographic Archives, Gillian Bardsley and Colin Corke), except for: p. 72 (bottom) Dorothy Knight; p. 174 (top) Yvonne Blakemore; p. 180 (top) John Baker of www.austinmemories.com; pp. 6, 184, 188 (top), 189 (top) Craig Holmes and St Modwen Properties; pp. 185, 186–7 St Modwen Properties; p. 190 (top) Pete Sloan, (bottom) Shaun Temple, both of the Longbridge Public Art Project.

Reproduction in any media not permitted without consent.

MAKING CARS AT
LONGBRIDGE
1905 TO THE PRESENT DAY

GILLIAN BARDSLEY AND COLIN CORKE
BRITISH MOTOR INDUSTRY HERITAGE TRUST

Cover illustrations. Front, top: An Austin Seven competes in the Spreadeagle Hill Climb for the Gordon England Cup in 1924; *bottom:* Early 'Minis' on the production line in CAB 1 *c.* 1959. *Back:* Robots welding Rover 200/400 bodies in New West Works.

First published 2006
This new edition published 2016

The History Press
Stroud, Gloucestershire, GL5 2QG
www.thehistorypress.co.uk

British Library Cataloguing in Publication Data.
A catalogue record for this book is available from the British Library.

ISBN 978 0 7509 6529 3

Typesetting and origination by The History Press
Printed and bound in Great Britain by TJ International Ltd

Contents

Foreword

by Mike Murray, Senior Development Surveyor
at St Modwen Properties

It has been ten years since the gates of the MG Rover plant closed for the last time and therefore a fitting anniversary for Gillian Bardsley and Colin Corke to release this revised and updated edition of *Making Cars at Longbridge*. Two new chapters and a colour section are included in this latest version, which charts a century of car production at the plant through illustrations, photographs and captions. This 2015 edition includes a new finale, which encompasses St Modwen's work to regenerate the area in order to keep it at the forefront of industrial Britain, albeit with a new focus on technology and innovation.

I have worked at Longbridge for thirteen years now and was here when the closure was announced. I feel as if the area is as much in my blood as it was for those who worked on the assembly line of the car plant in its heyday. Undoubtedly Longbridge has been transformed since the time when it was Europe's biggest car plant that dominated the area, but the current success of Longbridge is about rebuilding the community and economy. Now, against all the odds, there is a tangible pride here in Longbridge again, with offices, industry, new houses, new shops, new parks, a new college and new infrastructure having been created: a community is taking shape.

Longbridge has and will continue to have a rich heritage, which is beautifully celebrated in this book; and I am delighted that *Making Cars at Longbridge* is now celebrating the area's rich future too.

Mike Murray in his office at Longbridge.

One
Welcome to Longbridge

From its inception as a car factory in 1905, Longbridge was the heart of a vibrant community. Throughout its history it proudly welcomed visitors through its gates to see what went on inside. We extend the same invitation to you.

'Q gate', 1965.

LONGBRIDGE WORKS

are situate about seven miles from
Birmingham, on the main Bristol
Road, at the foot of the famous
Lickey Hills, one of the prettiest and
healthiest districts in the Midlands.

GENERAL VIEW OF LONGBRIDGE WORKS.

This 1908 brochure emphasised the factory as much as its products. The smoke pouring from the chimneys
sat rather uncomfortably alongside the claim that it lay in 'one of the prettiest and healthiest districts of the
Midlands'. The pure air, away from the pollution churned out by rival businesses in the city, was claimed to
benefit the paintwork. Austins were offered to customers in chassis form so they could choose their preferred
bodywork from a range of coachbuilt styles.

Visitors are very welcome at Longbridge, where they can see the complete manufacture of Britain's dependable cars. Arrangements can be made for parties or individuals, and those wishing to take advantage of the excellent facilities offered, should apply to the Reception Officer, Longbridge. During 1964 nearly 16,300 visitors were received.

To Visitors

Greeting!

IN handing you this booklet The Austin Motor Company expresses the hope that an insight into the history, activities and ideals of the organisation will enable you to appreciate the Company's desire to set the standard in Motor Car production. The traditions of the Company are such that nothing but the best is good enough. As efficiency is the keynote of the Longbridge factory so is it the characteristic of Austin performance in every part of the world.

H. Austin

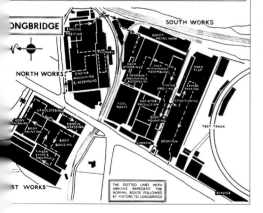

A ROUTE GUIDE TO
LONGBRIDGE
WEST, NORTH & SOUTH WORKS.

recurring theme through the years was the factory visit, offered to employees, their families, potential purchasers and any interested member of the public. This publicity material ranges from a personal greeting by Herbert Austin himself to the 'MG Rover Xperience' which was still on offer in 2005.

Longbridge, 1973. This page shows the heart of the pre-war factory complex. From West Works (bottom left) a conveyor carries bodyshells over the main Bristol Road into South Works. North Works is to the left beyond the arc of the railway line. A roundabout sits opposite the original entrance, 'K Gate'. Post-war development shifted the focus of the site to the area shown on the next page.

The circle of the old Flying Ground encompasses two Car Assembly Buildings (top) plus Administration, Design and Showroom blocks (bottom). Opposite the park is the main entrance, 'Q Gate'. Just above is the flat roof of the multi-storey car park. Top right is Flight Shed, a wartime development along with East Works which is just out of shot and across the Birmingham City boundary in Worcestershire.

1906 – the original entrance to the former White & Pike Works resembled a farm gate. A muddy path led to the turreted building where Herbert Austin set up his office. A distinctive bell tower called workers to and from their shifts and the water tower bore the Austin Motor Company name.

1950 – the wooden fence had given way to an iron structure. Workers poured through both 'IN' and 'OUT' gates on foot at the end of their shift. The old offices were still straight ahead, though they had gained a second storey and were flanked by substantial buildings to either side.

1967 – 'Gate K' had a guard house and a new set of iron gates. Though still in use it no longer served as the main entrance. The water tower and its obsolete Austin logo were still prominent from this angle. The building to the left survived but the block where Austin set up his office had gone.

2005 – 'K Gate' had been locked for years. The building to the left was one of the oldest remaining structures. To the right stood South Engineering Block, an impressive 1950s construction. The conveyor bridge swung behind into the machine shop which carried an illuminated 'MG Rover' sign.

1931 – the original Austin Seven (launched in 1922) is shown being built on a moving assembly line. Mass production techniques were still being developed throughout this period, pioneered by Austin's friend Henry Ford.

1951 – and a new Austin Seven 'A30' arrived using the unitary construction method which dispensed with a separate chassis frame. This technology caused a fundamental shift in the way a car was assembled.

1959 – the Austin Seven reached its third incarnation, though it would soon be renamed the Mini. Working by hand on the exposed seams of the bodyshell was still the order of the day.

1980 – the last small family car to come from Longbridge was the Austin Metro, also famous for the robots installed to build it. The mechanical arms reaching into the bodyframe automatically achieved the intricate welds with accuracy and speed.

Austin, 1951.

BMC, 1957.

British Leyland, 1969.

British Leyland, 1973.

Austin Morris, 1979 (as revealed in 2003).

Longbridge Technology Park, 2005.

During the 1950s a hoarding was erected which greeted those approaching the Longbridge Works from the direction of Birmingham for the next half century. The messages informed passers-by about the purpose of the factory but the presentation changed with each new identity it adopted.

Two

The Austin Dream
1905–1919

Herbert Austin hung the motto 'Most everything worthwhile is born of some dreamer's dream' on his office wall to inspire him. The mantelpiece of his fireplace was decorated with shells as a reminder of the factory's contribution to the war effort which earned him a knighthood.

Herbert Austin's office as preserved in the 1950s.

When Herbert Austin founded the Austin Motor Company in 1905, aged thirty-nine, he was already a well established engineer and businessman. As a young man of seventeen he had left for Australia and in time joined the Wolseley Sheep Shearing Machine Company as a trouble-shooter to solve its problems of poor quality manufacture. His advice to them was to set up a factory in England. After ten years overseas he returned in 1893, a mature young man with a wife and family, to become Managing Director of the new Birmingham Works. He took an interest in the new 'autocar' technology and built two experimental cars in 1895/6. On the strength of this, Wolseley agreed to go into motor manufacture and he became head of this enterprise too. But in 1905, ostensibly due to a dispute over engine design, he left to set up a business in his own name.

He found a disused factory at Longbridge, built some ten years earlier by tin printers White & Pike about seven miles outside Birmingham. It offered the advantages of extensive existing workshops, a pleasant rural location and easy rail access. His good reputation quickly attracted backers who provided the money needed to buy and re-equip the factory. In April 1906 he successfully tested the first Austin car, a 25/30hp with rudimentary bodywork. He had already obtained advanced orders at the Motor Show and was soon offering a wide range of body styles as well as associated products such as lighting sets.

The motor car in its infancy was a luxury product and early production concentrated on larger vehicles. A single cylinder two seater 7hp car was built in association with Swift in 1910 but it was not a sales success. Austin also developed a special line in taxis and moved into lorry production in 1913. Herbert enjoyed motor sport, which was an excellent promotional tool, and his cars did well in competition. The Austin Motor Company adopted an elaborate winged wheel as its symbol to express 'freedom' and 'style'. This was fixed to the cars as a badge as well as being used in publicity material. Much was made of the impressive factory and customers were encouraged to come and view it for themselves.

In 1910 Herbert Austin took up residence at Lickey Grange, a large house with 200 acres of parkland reflecting the success of his ventures so far. The Works employed over 2,500 people by 1914, the year Austin became a public limited liability company thus increasing its working capital. The start of the First World War that year interrupted this steady progress. Shells were produced in vast quantity, alongside lorries, ambulances and aircraft. The need for military production caused the factory to grow at a phenomenal rate. The original White & Pike buildings became the focus of South Works. New areas known as North Works and West Works were added. A Flying Ground covering over seventy acres was also created by flattening the top of a hill inside the complex. The workforce peaked at 22,000 during the course of the war leading to housing shortages. Austin's solution was to erect an estate of prefabricated timber bungalows, imported from Michigan, near the factory which would become known as the 'Austin Village', supplementing two residential hostels.

The war brought tragedy to the Austin family when their only son, Vernon, was killed in France by a sniper early in 1915. Herbert was nevertheless proud to receive a knighthood for his great contribution to the war and faced the task of returning to peacetime production with optimism.

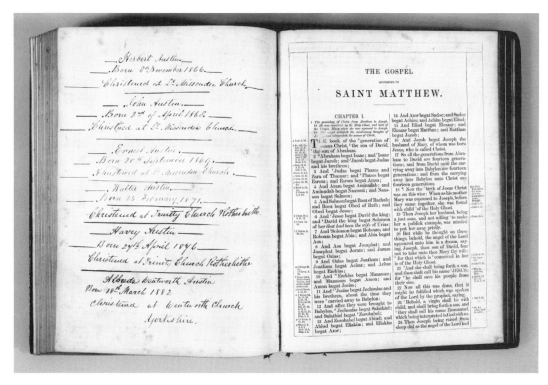

Herbert Austin came from a farming family and grew up in Yorkshire. His father, John, wrote the names and dates of birth of his children in the family Bible, appropriately choosing the blank page opposite St Matthew's recital of the genealogy of Jesus.

As a young man (right) he trained to be an architect but changed his mind in favour of engineering. After the family received a visit from dashing Australian émigré Uncle Walter (left), Herbert accompanied him to Australia where he eventually joined the Wolseley Sheep Shearing Machine Company.

The Wolseley Voiturette

Price - - £225.

Very Powerful Motor.

＊

Simple and Efficient Mechanism.

Perfect Cooling
. . and . .
Lubricating Systems.

＊

Centre of Gravity, Low.

VERY SILENT. LITTLE VIBRATION. MOST COMFORTABLE TO RIDE IN.

Every Detail Carefully Thought Out. Nothing Flimsy.

In 1893 Austin returned to Britain to manage a new factory in Birmingham. He began to experiment with 'autocars' and persuaded Wolseley to build one for sale in 1899. He appeared personally in early adverts (on the left), steering with a tiller rather than a wheel which had not yet become standard.

Austin (extreme left) was a keen participant in motor sport. Racing driver Charles Jarrott (next to Austin) pushed his Wolseley 'Beetle' to the start line at the Isle of Man Tourist Trophy in 1904.

Works –

Estimate of expenditure in 1st 3 months

Works –		
Legal charges –		150
Setting works in order		150
Signs furniture &c		100
Rates –		30
Repairs –		25 ? 100
		455
Plant – say –		3,000
Purchases –		2,500
Wages –		3000
Salaries –		500
Advertising		250
Exhibitions Trials &c .		100
Catalogues Stationery		150
Travelling		100
		9,055
Life ins[urance]		1,800
If works taken on Mortgage –		3,000
(leaving £5,000)		13,855

If K. or other lends – 5,000 pay him 6% interest £300
10,000 " = 600
and give him ⅛ share on
nett profits for 3 years
15,000 – 900
and give him ¼ share
on do for 3 yrs

loan to be for 5 years or at my option to pay
off altogether in 3 years ✓,

Austin decided to go into business on his own account. A detailed set of documents, dated 6 September 1905, contains this balance sheet setting out the finance required to start a motorcar factory. It included a loan from his friend, 'K' – Frank Kayser. Subsequent pages in his handwriting reveal that he had already located and valued the Longbridge Works and that 'very little alteration would be required to make the various shops suitable and a start could be made in about 3 weeks after taking possession'.

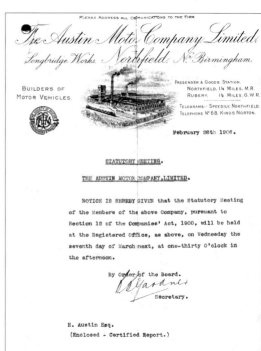

Berwood Grove.
Erdington.

October 26th 1905.

Mr. P. E. Provost.

c/o Mrs Sibson.

3, St. Martin's Place,

Broad Street,

Birmingham.

Dear Sir,

In reply to your letter of the 24th instant, I shall be glad if you can meet me at 11. O'clock on Saturday next at my new Works at Northfield. The Works are situated about 1¼ miles from Northfield Station, on the Bromsgrove Road, and anyone will direct you to them by mentioning "White & Pike's old place".

Yours faithfully,

PLEASE ADDRESS ALL COMMUNICATIONS TO THE FIRM

The Austin Motor Company Limited.

Longbridge Works. Northfield. N. Birmingham.

BUILDERS OF
MOTOR VEHICLES.

PASSENGER & GOODS STATION.
NORTHFIELD, 1¼ MILES, M.R.
RUBERY, 1½ MILES, G.W.R.

TELEGRAMS:— SPEEDILY, NORTHFIELD.
TELEPHONE N° 68, KINGS NORTON.

February 28th 1906.

STATUTORY MEETING.

THE AUSTIN MOTOR COMPANY, LIMITED.

NOTICE IS HEREBY GIVEN that the Statutory Meeting of the Members of the above Company, pursuant to Section 12 of the Companies' Act, 1900, will be held at the Registered Office, as above, on Wednesday the seventh day of March next, at one-thirty O'clock in the afternoon.

By Order of the Board.

Secretary.

H. Austin Esq.

(Enclosed - Certified Report.)

In October 1905 he wrote from his home address to another potential investor asking for a meeting at 'White & Pike's old place'. By February 1906 (right) this had been transformed into the 'Austin Motor Company Limited Longbridge Works' with its own impressive letterhead.

Shortly afterwards the first 25/30hp 'Austin' car was completed and he drove it out of the factory onto the Lickey Road for tests. The surrounding area would change considerably in later years as a result of his efforts.

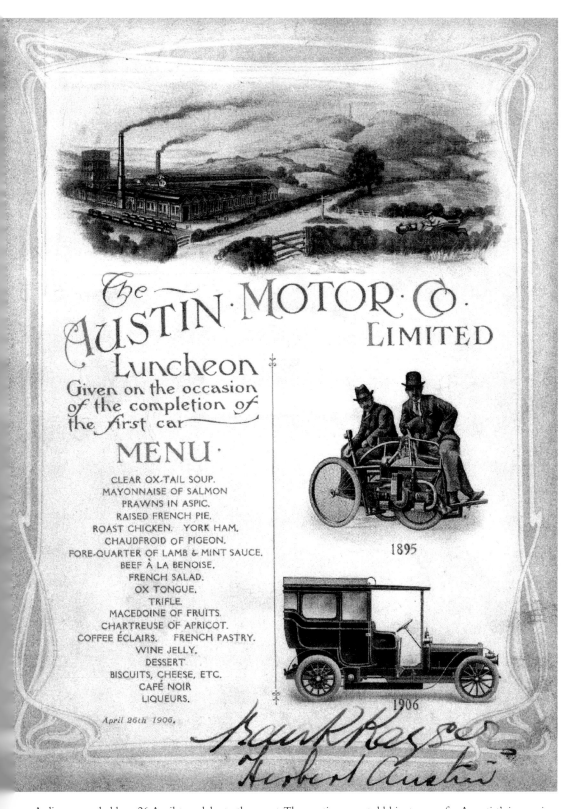

The AUSTIN·MOTOR·Co· LIMITED

Luncheon

Given on the occasion of the completion of the first car

MENU·

CLEAR OX-TAIL SOUP.
MAYONNAISE OF SALMON
PRAWNS IN ASPIC.
RAISED FRENCH PIE.
ROAST CHICKEN. YORK HAM.
CHAUDFROID OF PIGEON.
FORE-QUARTER OF LAMB & MINT SAUCE.
BEEF À LA BENOISE.
FRENCH SALAD.
OX TONGUE.
TRIFLE.
MACEDOINE OF FRUITS.
CHARTREUSE OF APRICOT.
COFFEE ÉCLAIRS.   FRENCH PASTRY.
WINE JELLY.
DESSERT
BISCUITS, CHEESE, ETC.
CAFÉ NOIR
LIQUEURS.

April 26th 1906.

1895

1906

A dinner was held on 26 April to celebrate the event. The exotic menu told his story so far. An artist's impression of the Works emphasised the rural setting and included a determined racer hurtling downhill. Herbert appears at the tiller of one of his early prototypes with his brother Harry. The original Austin car is shown at the bottom. He and Kayser signed this copy of the menu as a memento.

LONGBRIDGE WORKS.

Early catalogues made as much of 'advanced' production methods as of the vehicles they produced. This montage of 1908 shows chassis and engine erecting processes, contrasting with the bodyshop which continued to use traditional coachbuilding techniques.

In 1908 Austin built four 100hp racers to contest the prestigious French Grand Prix. Number 18 looked rather lonely in the paddock in the late afternoon sun. It was one of only two British cars to finish, and one of its drivers would later become famous as Lord Brabazon of Tara.

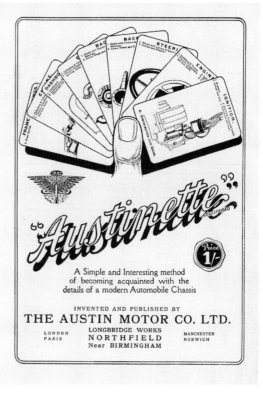

By 1909 Austin, as a 'British design pioneer', warranted a caricature in 'Automotor Journal'. The company was always looking for new promotional methods and came up with a set of playing cards to help people understand the workings of the 'modern automobile chassis'.

The driver of this 15hp Austin was not chauffeur to a wealthy owner but an employee of 'Urban Taxicabs Ltd' awaiting a fare in 1909. The company were early entrants into the important taxi cab market.

Whether for hire or purchase, cars were still a costly luxury. A 1911 Austin tyre and wheel brochure illustrated the ease with which a young servant could change the pneumatic tyre on a car fitted with a removable rim.

THE Austin ADVOCATE.

Vol. II. No. 1.   November, 1912.

The 'Austin Advocate' (later to become the 'Austin Magazine') was an early in-house publication. This cover extravagantly demonstrates its purpose – to glorify the factory and its products.

Part of the Longbridge ethos was to manufacture every part of the vehicle on site, so it employed a wide variety of trades in specialist areas. In the heat treatment plant, the operator kept a safe distance by using a long-handled metal stick to open and close the furnace.

Equally worrying were the gas mantles hanging from the roof struts over the ash frames of the body shop. Austin published separate catalogues for customers to match their preferred body style with their choice of chassis/engine combination.

A well-to-do mother and her children are ferried from the theatre in a 15hp 4-cylinder snub nosed Town Carriage of 1911. The compact layout was designed specifically for 'crowded streets and awkward spaces'. Little did they know of the demands which would be made by the congested streets of the future.

As the factory grew in prosperity Herbert Austin (front row under the clock in a bowler hat) gathered his supporters for a group picture. These buildings were the heart of the original factory with its distinctive water and bell towers.

Austin's son Vernon (without cap) inherited his father's love of motor sport and joined H. Kendall as riding-mechanic on a 20hp Austin at the Alpine Trials in June 1914. The company issued a brochure to celebrate their feats, including an artist's impression of the difficult terrain (below left).

Sadly he did not live to inherit the business as his father hoped. Only nine months after his adventures in the Alps, Vernon was killed in action at La Bassée on the Western Front aged only twenty-one. This is the memorial from the church in Canterbury where he was buried.

Like the rest of British industry, Longbridge had to dedicate itself to the war effort and began to turn out battle vehicles and munitions, in this case adapters for shells.

So many young men were dying on the battlefield that conscription was introduced in 1915. Out of necessity young women were allowed into the engineering departments for the first time.

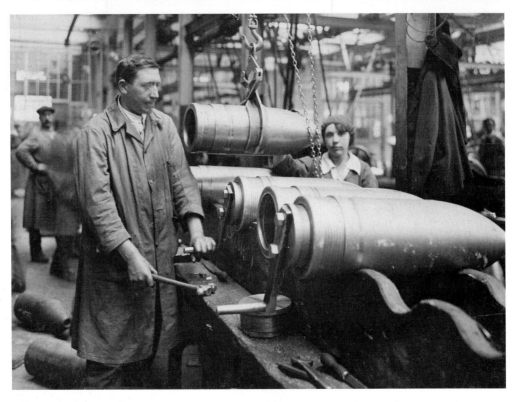

Experience and youth – an older worker taught one of the young women recruits how to put the finishing touches to a shell.

Almost eight million shells had been manufactured by the end of the war, introducing the concept of 'mass production' to the factory. The War Ministry sent its inspectors to check the finished items and the impressive response to government demands earned Longbridge great accolades.

During the First World War, aero technology had advanced to a stage at which it was becoming essential to the war effort. Austin produced around 2,000 aeroplanes most of them of the SE5A type pictured here.

The 'Austin Village' as it was in the 1940s. Around 200 wooden bungalows were built in 1917 from prefabricated kits imported from Michigan, together with some brick-built houses. Intended to solve the accommodation problems of the expanding workforce, each house initially had at least seven inhabitants.

DATED..*n.* *7 Feb.*..1918.

AGREEMENT

IN

RESPECT OF

37. CENTRAL AVENUE

LONGBRIDGE ESTATE

NORTHFIELD

FOR HOUSE ON ESTATE TO BE USED AS A

POLICE STATION.

THE AUSTIN MOTOR CO LTD

AND

THE LORD MAYOR ALDERMEN

AND CITIZENS OF THE

CITY OF BIRMINGHAM.

SCHEDULE.

Porch.	Chemical fire extinctor and hooks therefor.
Living Room.	Gas pendant burner globe and mantle. Two green Holland roller blinds. Two hot water radiators.
Pantry.	One Green Holland roller blind.
Kitchen.	Gas bracket burner globe and mantle. Two Green Holland roller blinds. Dwarf dresser containing two drawers and cupboard. White porcelain enamelled sink with grooved drainer and hot and cold supply taps. Gas heated washing boiler. Gas cooker with usual equipment. Flap table. Hot water radiator with valve.
Back Bedroom.	Gas bracket burner globe and mantle. Green Holland roller blind. Hot water radiator with valve.
Bathroom.	Gas bracket with burner. Green Holland roller blind. White porcelain enamelled bath with hot and cold supply taps. W.C. Set complete.
Middle Bedroom.	Gas bracket burner globe and mantle. Green Holland roller blind. Hot water radiator.
Front Bedroom.	Gas bracket burner globe and mantle. Green Holland roller blind. Hot water radiator.
Heating Chamber.	Domestic hot water boiler (circuit in connection)
Outside.	Galvanized dust bin with conical cover. Larch line post.

The estate quickly gained its own police station. The document approving a change of use provided a fascinating inventory of the equipment to be found in each house, with unusual luxuries such as gas lighting and cooker, central heating, hot and cold running taps, and a fully fitted indoor bathroom.

The early factory was easily recognised by a chimney and the water tower labelled 'The Austin Motor Co Ltd'. The railway line provided easy access, crossing a wide bridge over the river Rea on its way to the Works.

The demands of the war led to a phase of building expansion, financed largely by the government in recognition of the efficiency with which Austin was meeting their needs. In September 1916 work was underway on a new Howitzer shell plant in an area which would become known as North Works.

Though civilian production had been halted, the military still needed vehicles such as these 2–3-ton Royal Navy lorries proceeding from the Works along the Lickey Road on their way to service.

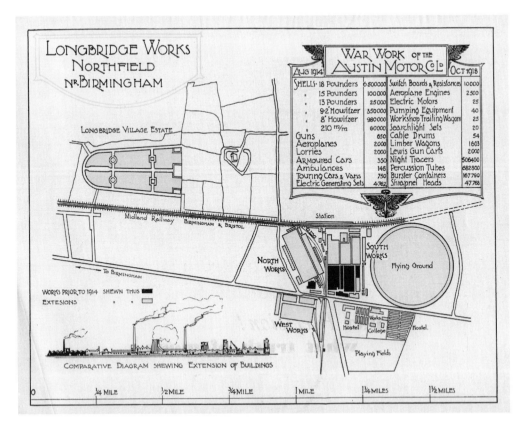

LONGBRIDGE WORKS NORTHFIELD NR BIRMINGHAM

WAR WORK OF THE AUSTIN MOTOR CO LD

AUG 1914		OCT 1918	
SHELLS- 18 Pounders	6,500,000	Switch Boards & Resistances	10,000
„ 15 Pounders	100,000	Aeroplane Engines	2,500
„ 13 Pounders	25,000	Electric Motors	25
„ 9·2" Howitzer	350,000	Pumping Equipment	40
„ 8" Howitzer	980,000	Workshop Trailing Wagons	25
„ 210 m/m	60,000	Searchlight Sets	20
Guns	650	Cable Drums	54
Aeroplanes	2,000	Limber Wagons	1,603
Lorries	2,000	Lewis Gun Carts	2,000
Armoured Cars	350	Night Tracers	506,400
Ambulances	148	Percussion Tubes	682,800
Touring Cars & Vans	750	Burster Containers	167,790
Electric Generating Sets	4,762	Shrapnel Heads	47,768

LONGBRIDGE VILLAGE ESTATE

Midland Railway BIRMINGHAM & BRISTOL

To BIRMINGHAM

Station

NORTH WORKS

SOUTH WORKS

Flying Ground

WORKS PRIOR TO 1914 SHEWN THUS

EXTESIONS „

WEST WORKS

Hostel   Works College   Hostel

Playing Fields

COMPARATIVE DIAGRAM SHEWING EXTENSION OF BUILDINGS

| 0 | ¼ MILE | ½ MILE | ¾ MILE | I MILE | 1¼ MILES | 1½ MILES |

This map illustrates the expansion of the factory by 1918 and shows two hostels in addition to the 'Longbridge Village Estate' underlining how difficult it had been to sustain such rapid growth. A chart justly boasts of the wartime productivity which had been achieved.

Three

Dependable Austin
1919–1939

In the post-war period the Austin Motor Company suffered severe difficulties followed by a strong recovery. But a constant feature was the use of the slogan 'as dependable as an Austin' to promote its products in print and on film which provided an accurate description of the qualities of their cars.

why. . . AS DEPENDABLE AS AN AUSTIN?

The Sixteen Gearbox—in first gear

WHAT *Precision!*
what truth of mesh !

 AUSTIN

Read the
AUSTIN
Magazine
FOURPENCE
EVERY
MONTH

AS . DEPENDABLE . AS . AN . AUSTIN

The Austin Motor Co. Ltd., Longbridge, Birmingham. Showrooms, also Service Station for the Austin Seven : 479-483
Oxford Street, London, W.1. Showrooms and Service Station : Holland Park Hall, W.11.

From 1918 to 1924 Herbert Austin served as Unionist MP for Kings Norton (the Birmingham constituency which included Longbridge). Business success was more elusive as the world economy slumped into depression. The peacetime plan was to build civilian aircraft and tractors, while concentrating car production on the large Austin Twenty. Unfortunately, though it was well engineered, it failed to attract sufficient sales. The overheads of the expanded factory were exposing the company to severe financial problems. Despite energetic attempts to raise extra funds to keep the company afloat, Receivers had to be appointed in April 1921. Austin lost sole control of his company and became chairman of a Board of Directors.

Happily the reconstruction plan worked. The Twenty was supplemented by a smaller Austin Twelve which brought the company back into profit. The Austin Seven completed the recovery. Instead of a crude 'cyclecar' which was little more than a glorified motorcycle with three or four wheels, this Baby Austin was a proper car in miniature. From its introduction in 1922 it enjoyed remarkable popularity, both as family transport and in motor sport. It was even built overseas in the United States, France, Germany and (unofficially) Japan.

In the hostile economic climate of the 1920s many manufacturers and suppliers went under. Austin emerged from its financial problems to become a dominant force alongside Morris Motors, the company founded by William Morris (later Lord Nuffield) at Cowley near Oxford. Their philosophies were very different and this influenced the culture of their rival enterprises. Morris built his empire on the assembly of cars from bought-in components. Austin practised on-site manufacture of the whole vehicle and its parts as far as possible. This created a tremendous breadth of skills within the Longbridge workforce though it also meant high overheads and made it difficult to cost the building of a car accurately.

Austin used magazines and films to generate what would now be called 'brand loyalty' from dealers and customers. The slogan 'as dependable as an Austin' reflected the company's reputation for well-built but rather unexciting designs. The charismatic Austin Seven was sold using much cheekier and more imaginative material. But as the design aged and grew more refined, with elegant models such as the Ruby, the Pearl and the Top Hat, there seemed to be little inspiration for a successor. A Big Seven failed to supplant it. The Austin Eight, launched in 1938 was more successful but lacked the character of the Baby Austin.

Throughout this period constant updating of production methods and equipment was essential to stay ahead. The recruitment of Leonard Lord in 1938 was therefore an important moment. Lord, prime mover behind the modernisation of Morris, was looking for a new opportunity after a disagreement with Lord Nuffield. At Longbridge he continued to update both the factory and its products. He also allowed smoking by the workforce, much to the annoyance of Herbert Austin who loathed the habit.

Austin's personal progress continued too. In 1936 he made a large donation to the work of Lord Rutherford at Cambridge University to support scientific research which eventually contributed to splitting the atom. He was created Lord Austin later that year. Most significant, to himself and the company, would be the key role he played in preparations for another global conflict which was approaching fast by 1939.

After the loss of their son, the Austins celebrated a happier event on 14 October 1918 when their eldest daughter, Irene, married Captain Arthur Waite. Her Australian husband was a successful racing driver and would become a member of the Longbridge management team.

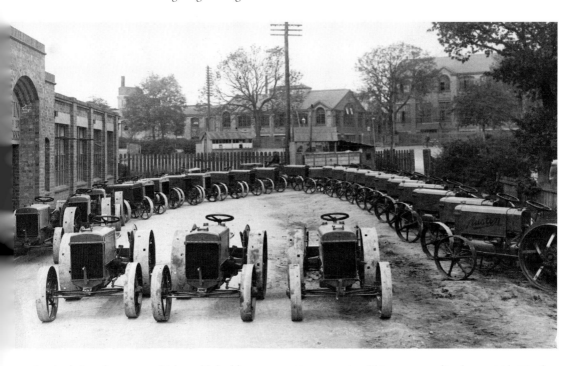

Austin designed a tractor which could double up as a stationary engine. This group was lined up outside North Works, with West Works visible in the background. They were also manufactured at a subsidiary factory in France.

His new son-in-law organised a publicity stunt, ferrying visitors to see the re-organised factory using a day's output of Austin Twenties. The decision to offer only this model of car proved disastrous when the price had to be increased at the same time as the world economy went into freefall.

SIR HERBERT AUSTIN, M.P.

THE AUSTIN MOTOR CO. LTD.

BUILDERS OF PRIVATE AND COMMERCIAL MOTOR VEHICLES
AGRICULTURAL TRACTORS, ELECTRIC LIGHTING & POWER PLANTS

DEPOTS.
LONDON MANCHESTER, PARIS & BRUSSELS.

GOODS TO BE { LONGBRIDGE NORTH SIDINGS, RUBERY } AS ORDERED
CONSIGNED TO { LONGBRIDGE SOUTH SIDINGS, RUBERY }
{ LONGBRIDGE WEST SIDINGS, RUBERY }
STATION FOR PASSENGERS NORTHFIELD.

LONGBRIDGE WORKS
NORTHFIELD
BIRMINGHAM.

TELEPHONE: KINGS NORTON 111/2 230/4 236/7.
CENTRAL 4140/1 AND 4143.
TELEGRAMS: "SPEEDILY NORTHFIELD."
CABLES A.B.C. 5TH EDITION & PRIVATE.

28th February, 1921.

Dear Sir (or Madam),

The Directors cannot too strongly impress upon you the necessity for reading the following particulars.

The estimates of the finances required by our business made a little over a year ago still hold good, but, owing to the difficult conditions prevailing, it has been found impossible to provide the £1,250,000 which it was proposed to bring into the Company in the form of Ordinary Shares at the time when the £1,500,000 Preferred Ordinary Shares were created.

During the whole of the past year the business has been carried on under very great difficulties and restrictions in consequence of the above shortage of capital, and the Directors have finally had to decide to make an issue of Debentures as the best and most economical means available at the present time to finance the increased trade of the Company.

The result of the issue is of the most vital importance to you as a Shareholder, and the Directors cannot carry on the business without this additional finance.

Yours faithfully,

H. Austin

Chairman and Managing Director,
AUSTIN MOTOR CO. LTD.

Herbert Austin served as MP for Kings Norton from 1918–24 but his company was in trouble. He needed to raise £1.5 million and issued a stark letter to existing shareholders begging for their assistance: 'the Directors cannot carry on the business without this additional finance'.

The Austin Motor Company Ld

BUILDERS OF PRIVATE AND COMMERCIAL VEHICLES
AIRCRAFT & AIRCRAFT ENGINES, PETROL & PARAFFIN POWER PLANTS FOR ELECTRICITY AND OTHER PURPOSES

DEPÔTS:
LONDON, MANCHESTER,
PARIS & BRUSSELS.
STATION FOR PASSENGERS:
NORTHFIELD.

LONGBRIDGE WORKS,
NORTHFIELD.

BIRMINGHAM.

TELEPHONE: KINGS NORTON 230
PTE. BRANCH EXCHANGE
TELEGRAMS: "SPEEDILY, NORTHFIELD".
CABLES: A.B.C 5TH EDITION & PRIVATE.

24

ALL CORRESPONDENCE MUST BE ADDRESSED TO THE COMPANY AND NOT TO INDIVIDUALS

Our Ref

CONSIGN GOODS TO LONGBRIDGE (RUBERY), M.R. & G.W.R.

MR. A.W. JONES.   27th April 1921

     I have to inform you that owing to the
appointment of Sir Arthur Whinney as Receiver and Manager,
on the 26th inst. it necessarily follows that all
engagements with the Company are automatically terminated
on that date.

     I am also to inform you that from to-day
you are engaged by the Receiver and Manager of the Company –
the engagement to be subject to one week's notice on
either side.

[signature]

SECRETARY.

All efforts to raise the money failed. The company went into receivership on 26 April 1921, a poignant date marking the fifteenth anniversary of the dinner to celebrate the first test drive. The workforce was told that it was now employed by the Receiver, Sir Arthur Whinney, and not the Austin Motor Company.

The Austin Seven's arrival in 1922 was one factor which helped to restore prosperity. As can be seen from the chassis on the left it was a proper car on a small scale rather than a rudimentary tub with a motorcycle engine. The photo suggests that even a woman could drive such a vehicle.

The Baby Austin would become one of the most popular models of the 1920s and helped to make motoring affordable to the middle classes. The publicity (bottom left) stressed not only its cheapness but its ability to make life brighter for its lucky owners.

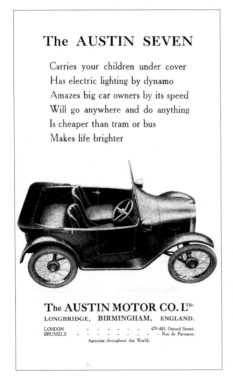

The AUSTIN SEVEN

Carries your children under cover
Has electric lighting by dynamo
Amazes big car owners by its speed
Will go anywhere and do anything
Is cheaper than tram or bus
Makes life brighter

The AUSTIN MOTOR CO. L™·
LONGBRIDGE, BIRMINGHAM, ENGLAND.

LONDON · · · · · · · 479-483, Oxford Street.
BRUSSELS · · · · · · · · - Rue de Parnasse.
Agencies throughout the World.

This 'dynasphere' was developed by 'Spherical Locomotion' and powered by an Austin Seven engine. It provided pleasure trips like the one, shown here, being enjoyed by the locals of Littlehampton in 1933.

Away from the production line, scientists mixed and tested various potions in the factory's laboratories in the search to maximise the performance of the company's products.

This vast army of administrative workers proves that the open plan office was not invented in the 1980s. Unlike the modern office, the desks all faced in the same direction but men and women were mixed together, filling in ledgers and cards by hand while the favoured few had access to a typewriter.

Above: By 1924, when this photograph of the Works was taken, the recovery of the business was well underway. The tower of Hollymoor Chapel was a distinctive mark on the horizon. The chimneys were still smoking across the countryside and an Austin Seven could be seen climbing the test hill next to the railway line.

The Way To Harley Street

Making a Start

Below: The same year this brochure was produced, illustrating the career progression of an average doctor through his choice of Austin cars on 'the way to Harley Street' and prosperity. Inevitably he started with an Austin Seven and moved onwards and upwards to the top of the range.

The Practice Grows

The Summit of Success

Expansion resumed in earnest. In 1931 a new Service Department was built, part of a block of offices whose impressive frontage stretched into the distance along the Lickey Road.

This fleet of Austin Ten-Fours on trade plates represented part of the first delivery on 18 April 1932, the day it was made public. This was Austin's rather belated reaction to the market demand for moderately sized 10hp vehicles.

The Board of Management in 1933, left to right: back, F.H. Pepper, Arthur Waite, T.D. Neal, R.G. Ash; front, E.L. Payton, Herbert Austin, and C.R.F. Englebach.

The employees also posed in their Sunday best as they waited on the railway station to board trains to take them on a Works outing, paid for by the company.

One revolution of the late 1920s was the introduction of the pressed steel process which gradually overtook traditional coachbuilding techniques. Dozens of carpenters and tinsmiths were replaced by huge presses capable of stamping out thousands of metal panels in a fraction of the time.

It was not just a matter of speed and quantity – the presses were capable of producing sweeping curves in shiny metal which it had not been possible to shape consistently over hand-built wooden frames. The operators were dwarfed by their machinery.

In the North Works foundry a brave blacksmith poured molten metal from a bucket into a mould to cast engine cylinder blocks. A 1933 brochure declared of this picture 'Longbridge is unique in its command of all the important facilities required for motor manufacture'.

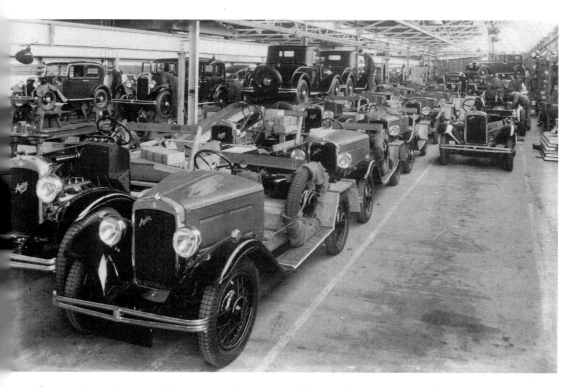

The pressed metal process did not necessarily produce uniformity. These Austin Tens still consisted of a basic chassis structure combined with a variety of possible body types.

In 1934 the 'Austin Magazine' published a series of 'factorygraphs' to illustrate the recent overhaul undergone by all production areas, explaining: 'the outstanding feature of this shop is the use made of modern conveyor systems to facilitate all the operations involved in chassis assembling. Our view can thus

ASSEMBLING CHASSIS AT LONGBRIDGE

show the confluence of assemblies which arrive in due order and in sufficient quantities from all quarters to ensure an uninterrupted flow of completed chassis.'

Herbert Austin kept his office in the oldest part of the factory. This photograph was taken for the 'Austin Magazine' in 1932. The caption indicated that he was on the phone to South Africa, showing the breadth of his business interests.

His office pictured in 1937, an impressive wood panelled room. The motto is still on the wall which also carries a barometer, a framed honour from the King of Belgium and a plaque commemorating the 1911 Turin Motor Show. The telephones have been updated.

After Austin's death the room was retained but his personal effects were removed. By the 1950s it looked stark and bare but the view remains with the Birmingham City Corporation water pumping works across the road clearly visible in the distance.

The office was moved due to demolition work during the 1950s. In 2002 it was reconstructed for the second time as part of a small Works museum. The window allowed visitors to look into the office from a viewing platform rather than providing a view for the 'guv'nor' to look out over his domain.

These shots of women polishing Austin Sevens are taken from the 1933 film 'This Progress'. An ambitious and expensive production by T.F. Aveling-Ginever, it used the pioneering technique of 'talkies' (synchronised sound) and featured a beautifully photographed period documentary.

Such films were for showing at dealers' evenings, held in local cinemas or on their own premises. Potential customers could not fail to be impressed by footage of the extensive railway network feeding the huge factory with raw materials.

This 20hp Austin of 1932 was specially fitted with ramps and folding seats to accommodate a wheelchair, in an age before complicated regulations about disabled access.

The Austin Heavy Twelve had been a mainstay of the product range since 1921. When the standard model was discontinued, a taxi version was maintained to feed a niche market where Austin was steadily gaining dominance.

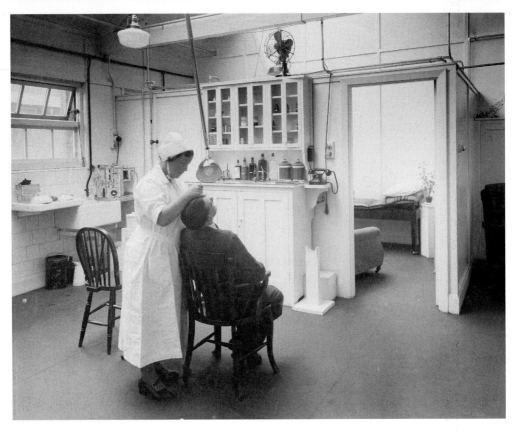

Health and welfare was provided for by professional support services such as firemen, policemen and nurses. In a well-equipped first-aid station, an efficient nurse tended to common ailments such as foreign bodies in the eye.

There was an extensive apprenticeship programme to nurture the skills of the future workforce. Austin himself inaugurated the Apprentices' Pavilion and Sports Ground by gamely pitching the first bowl down the skittle alley while appropriately retaining his bowler hat on his head.

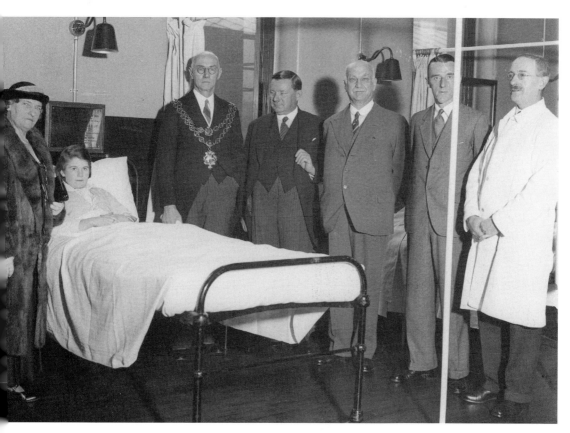

In 1935 the Austin Overseas Distributors honoured Sir Herbert by paying for a bed at the Birmingham General Hospital, of which he was chairman. He attended the dedication ceremony along with hospital staff, local dignitaries and a bemused young patient parked underneath the commemorative plaque.

Lickey Grange,
Nr. Bromsgrove.
April 29th 1936

Dear Mr. Baldwin,

I have for several years been watching the very valuable work done by Lord Rutherford & his colleagues at Cambridge in the realm of scientific research & knowing that, as Chancellor, you are keenly interested in obtaining sufficient funds with which to build, equip & endow a very much needed addition to the present resources, I shall be very pleased indeed to present securities to the value of approximately 250,000 for this purpose.

I may I request, if it is in order that my name will be associated with the extension

I am
Yours sincerely
H Austin

The Rt. Hon. Stanley Baldwin, M.P.
Prime Minister.
10, Downing Street
London S.W.1.

In 1936 Austin wrote to Stanley Baldwin offering a donation of £250,000 to support research into radiology at Cambridge University, of which the Prime Minister was Chancellor. The same year he became Baron Austin of Longbridge with his own crest and motto.

The Austin Seven was a versatile competition vehicle. Bert Hadley regularly drove for the Works Team and impressed at the famous Shelsley Walsh hill climb with an Austin twin cam. Even the driver seems to think the car is a little noisy.

Just before the war new recruit Leonard Lord introduced a range of new-style cars with raked windscreens, alligator bonnets and horizontal grilles. An Austin Ten undertook a challenge to visit the four corners of Britain within four days. Austin performed the duty of sealing the bonnet before it set off.

Four

Thanks for the Guns!
1936–1946

Like the rest of British industry, motor manufacturers once again had to suspend normal production and turn themselves over to the military effort when war was declared on Germany in 1939.

Thanks for the Guns!

Guns are still a vital need, and the Motor Industry will continue to make them until the day of Victory. Then, the Industry will whole-heartedly support the Government with well-founded plans for full employment.

THE MOTOR INDUSTRY
MANUFACTURE · DISTRIBUTION · MAINTENANCE

Production for Victory

Because of the experience gained during one major conflict, Austin knew the importance of being well prepared as another war began to seem inevitable. It was therefore appropriate when, in 1936, he became chairman of the 'Shadow Aero Engine Committee'. The remit of this government body was to plan extra manufacturing capacity in locations which would be relatively safe from attack. As a result Longbridge itself gained several new facilities for aircraft manufacture. Flight Shed was distinctive for its interior space incorporating an impressive roof structure which minimised the use of pillars. Close by was a new Aero Factory which would become known as East Works. The first aircraft built were Fairey Battles, a design which proved disappointing in service. Smaller planes could be flown from the old Flying Ground. Larger aircraft such as Stirling bombers were made as kits and transported to nearby Elmdon airport. As well as aircraft a wide variety of wartime products came out of Longbridge between 1939 and 1945, from military vehicles to jerricans.

As early as 1936 a series of tunnels was also being prepared, burrowing into the hillsides and linking the various parts of the factory. Ultimately the network covered over three miles. It was intended to shelter both the workforce and manufacturing operations in case of heavy bombing. In the event, the site's hilly terrain combined with the camouflage on the buildings, provided an effective disguise. Locals declared their astonishment to discover how difficult it was to make out the sprawling complex from the vantage point of the nearby Lickey Hills. This may have contributed to the fact that Longbridge suffered few air raids, meaning that the tunnels were never called into full use. Some of the workforce, however, were killed in a bomb attack during 1940 which greatly saddened Austin. The following year he died suddenly of a heart attack when thought to be making reasonable progress after a long bout of illness. His wife died almost exactly one year later and both are buried at Lickey Parish Church near their family home.

Though the chairmanship passed to the astute Ernest Peyton, it was the young and dynamic Leonard Lord who was now the power behind the throne. This would be an important factor as planning for peace-time production began. As early as 1944 the company announced its post-war range of cars which, of necessity, consisted of the 1939 models with minor modifications. The Austin Motor Company was one of the first to resume civilian production, returning chromium trim and gloss paint to its cars and exploring export opportunities with vigour. The wartime shadow factories were soon available for mainstream manufacture. In 1946 the 'millionth Austin', a top-of-the-range Sixteen, was celebrated with due ceremony, signed by the people who made it and retained for exhibition.

Leonard Lord, who became chairman in 1945, criticised the government, complaining of lack of support as the British motor industry attempted to recover in the face of continued shortages of fuel and materials. The government countered with the message 'export or die'. But market forces were not allowed to take effect. In the post-war period a series of Chancellors of the Exchequer embarked on a long-term policy of adjusting credit arrangements and taxation on new cars to manipulate demand in line with whatever economic strategy they were following at the time.

A GLIMPSE INTO "SHADOWLAND"

Disclosing the progress achieved with the Government Shadow Factory Scheme.

UNTIL recently much had been heard of the Government Shadow aircraft factory scheme, but it remained very much a shadow and little was known of the progress made with this measure of national defence, beyond the fact that five motor manufacturers, namely the Austin, Daimler, Humber, Rover and Standard concerns, were co-operating with the Air Ministry. Now the results of fifteen to eighteen months' work have been disclosed, to reveal how substantial the "shadow" has become.

The illustrations on this page give a convincing indication of this fact. They show various aspects of the Austin Aircraft works, the largest of the five so far erected. It covers 23 acres which, less than eighteen months ago, were undulating fields and farm lands.

In the Austin factory complete aeroplanes as well as engines will be—in fact, are now being—constructed.

The office block of the Austin Motor Company's new aircraft factory at Cofton Hacket, almost adjacent to the car factory at Longbridge.

This view taken from the railway sidings shows something of the extent of the new aircraft factory. Only two-thirds of the factory are visible—photographic limitations precluding a complete view.

An interior view of the new Austin aircraft factory, erected for the Air Ministry, which is over 500 yards in length.

This time Britain had readied itself for the outbreak of hostilities. In December 1937 the 'Austin Magazine' gave a 'Glimpse into Shadowland' revealing the extent of preparations at Longbridge. The Aero Factory which it described was later known as East Works.

The scene was deceptively peaceful as a solitary horse and cart wended its way past the heavily camouflaged Aero Factory. A wide swing door across the building allowed for the movement of aircraft.

In September 1938 Austin and the Secretary of State for Air waited for the first Fairey Battle to take off from the Flying Ground behind Flight Shed (far left). A crowd gathered outside the office block of the Aero Factory and curious onlookers hung out of the windows.

Austin took holidays in Germany and a version of the Austin Seven had been built there under licence by recently established BMW. It was therefore not out of the ordinary when German Chancellor, Adolf Hitler, visited the Austin stand during the 1935 Berlin Motor Show.

A rather more welcome companion was racing driver George Eyston. In 1939 they posed together with an example of an Austin lorry which marked the company's first heavy vehicle for some years and would prove useful in wartime.

In March 1939 King George V and Queen Elizabeth visited the Aero Assembly Hall. Works Director Leonard Lord accompanied the Queen, while Lord Austin and Carl Englebach escorted the King. Further back was Prime Minister Neville Chamberlain who was also MP for a Birmingham constituency.

The enthusiastic Longbridge workforce lined the route or perched on the Fairey Battles which were now being produced in quantity. The manufacture of aeroplanes required clear uninterrupted areas which created less claustrophobic spaces than the older buildings.

As well as the shadow factories, an extensive network of tunnels was begun in 1936. They provided air raid shelters and some housed manufacturing operations too. The Ministry of Supply visited the tunnel next to the Aero Factory.

These women were assembling crankcases for aero engines underneath Flight Shed. In the event, Longbridge was not heavily bombed.

In 1938 Winston Churchill visited Austin at the shadow factory. On the extreme right is Managing Director E.L. Payton and on the left Ronald Cartland, MP for Austin's old constituency of Kings Norton.

Despite his huge contribution, Herbert Austin would not live to see the end of this war. He died in May 1941 and his funeral procession was witnessed by crowds of employees as it passed the factory on its way to his final resting place at Lickey Parish Church.

THE NAVY MAINTAINS UNCEASING PATROL

UNTIL THE CLOUDS PASS
—WE. TOO. WILL KEEP
FULL SPEED AHEAD

Left: Propaganda posters were affixed to gratings and walls all over the factory to encourage the workforce to put in maximum effort. Many of these were devised by the Austin Publicity Department.

Below: Longbridge contributed examples of its propaganda to a Birmingham city centre display called 'Tell the War Worker' in 1943. The posters were more admonishing than inspirational, using slogans such as 'better never late' and 'absence makes the war last longer'.

In 1942 Charles de Gaulle, leader of the Free French forces, was invited to Longbridge, where he inspected their Civil Defence Service and Home Guard. The tin hats could have been part of the two and a half million produced at the factory.

Office life went on much the same as before. The men and women of the Buyers Office in 1942 administered the purchase of all the materials needed to fulfil government contracts.

At Longbridge high speed presses stamped out handles for some of the 650,000 jerricans produced. The operators do not appear to be required to protect their fashionable hair despite the huge wheels of the machinery. The cans were welded together at a subsidiary in South Wales.

Petrol tanks for Lancaster bombers were made in two sections and welded together. These women were cleaning the interior though one is sporting more sensible work wear than the other.

A young engineer applied intense concentration to his task on the Oerlikon machine gun magazine, which required great precision.

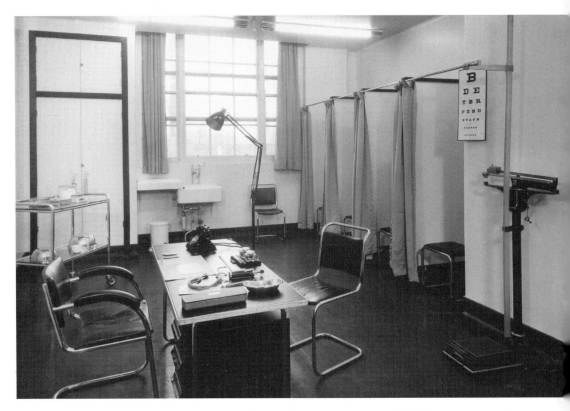

Meanwhile a medical department dedicated to Lord Austin's memory was opened. Health care was more than just a welfare issue, it made sound business sense to ensure the workforce was as fit as possible, especially in the days before the National Health Service.

Following Austin's death, Leonard Lord became the controlling influence at Longbridge. In 1944 he (front row fourth from right) and his trusted understudy, George Harriman (front row third from left), sat on either side of senior nurse Dorothy Day, a key member of the factory division of St John's nurses.

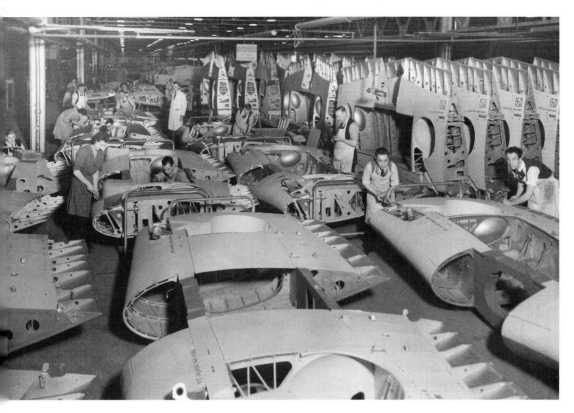

Longbridge also assembled the wing and centre section for the Miles Master training aircraft which would go on to be completed elsewhere.

The Stirling bomber was at the forefront of the air assault on Germany and later served as a troop carrier. In its early stages the fuselage resembled a large skeleton. Here the ribs of Duralumin alloy were almost ready to receive their outer skin.

In the eerie light of the Aero Factory, Stirling wings and assembled fuselages stretched as far as the eye could see. Making a plane of this size was a major undertaking. In total, 720 were produced.

The Flying Ground at Longbridge could not cope with larger aircraft, so after manufacture they were transported in sections to the new airport at Elmdon near Birmingham, where Austin had its own assembly and test sheds.

In the Austin Flight Shed at Elmdon the engineer was dwarfed by a Lancaster bomber starboard wing carrying a Merlin engine and propeller. His task was to test the operation of the undercarriage with special hydraulic equipment.

The Longbridge Home Guard and Civil Defence Services continued to keep themselves prepared for duty, undertaking regular training exercises throughout the war.

Austin made military vehicles such as these, in convoy outside the camouflaged factory. The Austin Ten Utility or 'Tilly' led the way, followed by a K2 ambulance and '4x4' trucks.

AUGUST, 1945

4 D.

VOL. 18
NO. 11

The *Austin* MAGAZINE
AND ADVOCATE

The 'Austin Magazine' marked the end of war in Europe with a victory cover in August 1945. The first post-war vehicles, gleaming with chrome and glossy paint, were revivals of the production halted in 1939. Alongside sat a line of khaki military lorries and Red Cross ambulances which would soon be phased out. Genuine post-war designs would take longer to reach the tracks.

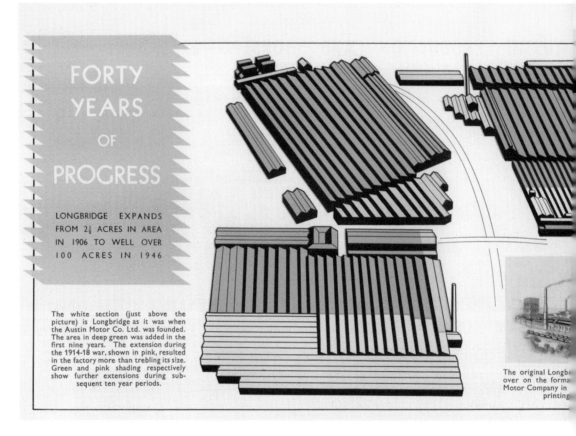

FORTY
YEARS
OF
PROGRESS

LONGBRIDGE EXPANDS
FROM 2¼ ACRES IN AREA
IN 1906 TO WELL OVER
100 ACRES IN 1946

The white section (just above the picture) is Longbridge as it was when the Austin Motor Co. Ltd. was founded. The area in deep green was added in the first nine years. The extension during the 1914-18 war, shown in pink, resulted in the factory more than trebling its size. Green and pink shading respectively show further extensions during subsequent ten year periods.

The original Longbr...
over on the forma...
Motor Company in...
printing...

In 1946 Austin celebrated not just the end of the war but also its fortieth anniversary. 'Forty Years of Progress' showed how the Works had expanded during that period. It was soon even bigger as the shadow factories became available for civilian production.

The end of conflict did not bring an immediate end to austerity. The motor industry suffered particularly from fuel shortages, and workers were encouraged to sign a petition asking for a more generous personal fuel allowance to aid the industry's recovery.

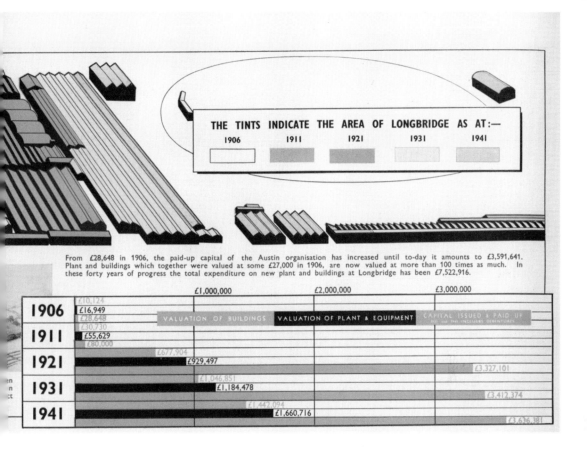

THE TINTS INDICATE THE AREA OF LONGBRIDGE AS AT:—
1906   1911   1921   1931   1941

From £28,648 in 1906, the paid-up capital of the Austin organisation has increased until to-day it amounts to £3,591,641. Plant and buildings which together were valued at some £27,000 in 1906, are now valued at more than 100 times as much. In these forty years of progress the total expenditure on new plant and buildings at Longbridge has been £7,522,916.

Year	VALUATION OF BUILDINGS	VALUATION OF PLANT & EQUIPMENT	CAPITAL ISSUED & PAID UP
1906	£10,124	£16,949	£28,648
1911	£30,730	£55,629	£80,000
1921	£677,904	£929,497	£3,327,101
1931	£1,046,851	£1,184,478	£3,412,374
1941	£1,442,094	£1,660,716	£3,636,381

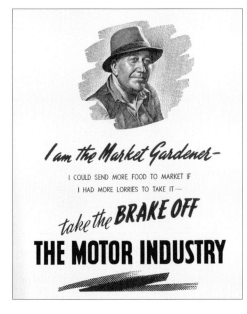

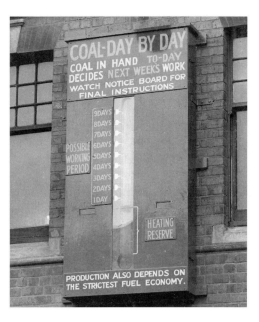

Press advertisements gave the same message. In the severe winter of 1945/6 Leonard Lord had an electronic board placed on the factory wall to demonstrate how coal rationing was hampering the productivity needed for the recovery of the damaged national economy.

When the Millionth Austin was built on 25 June 1946 the company staged an 'Austin Progress Convention' in the showroom. This Austin Sixteen (centre) was retained for the Works collection while cars 999,999 and 1,000,001 (to left and right of photograph) were allocated to employees by ballot.

Export was a priority to restock the nation's coffers. Longbridge was in a good position to respond quickly. An assembly area was turned over to export packing. Men used spray guns and stencils to apply patriotic lettering, with little more protection from the fumes than a floppy hat.

Five

Austin of England
1946–1959

'Austin of England' weathered post-war austerity to enter a period of renewed expansion. The state-of-the-art Car Assembly Building was opened with a fanfare from the King's Own Royal Regiment. The logo emblazoned on the building was also attached to the cars produced inside.

Opening of the new Chassis or Car Assembly Building (CAB) on 19 July 1951.

The company now styled itself 'Austin of England', reflecting its part in the massive export drive which was now required of industry to shore up the shell-shocked British economy. At home, only essential users such as doctors could jump the long waiting lists for a new car. Some cars were exported complete, others as Complete Knock Down (CKD) kits to be assembled locally in an effort to overcome national restrictions. An agreement with Nissan to assemble the A40 in Japan under licence was one of the most interesting examples. The first new design was the Sheerline of 1947, a prestige car which introduced the 'Flying A' bonnet mascot that characterised Austins of this period. In 1946 Austin acquired the coachbuilder Vanden Plas to build their luxury cars. A little later it began to collaborate with Donald Healey to produce a series of successful sportscars known as Austin-Healeys. Austin also made a small two-seater for the American company, Nash (later American Motors) sold in the US as the Metropolitan.

The Morris Minor led Lord Nuffield's post-war range, designed by Alec Issigonis who was building a reputation for innovativeness. Though Austin's products were more traditional, they were very successful at tapping overseas markets. One factor was publicity officer Alan Hess who had a broadcasting background. His imaginative stunts included eye-catching attempts on speed and endurance records. Austin re-entered the small car market at the end of 1951 with a new Austin Seven 'A30'. This car used the modern technique of unitary construction, dispensing with a separate chassis frame. It also marked the first appearance of the versatile A-series engine design which would remain in production for nearly fifty years.

The post-war period also saw a burst of site development based on the Flying Ground. In 1948 a new Administration Block was built which, in the Cold War era, was rapidly christened the 'Kremlin'. It was joined in 1951 by a new Chassis or Car Assembly Building (CAB). At the same time, market forces were pushing the two rivals Morris and Austin towards each other and in 1952 they agreed to merge. Lord Nuffield became chairman, but vice-chairman Leonard Lord ensured that Longbridge was the headquarters and dominant partner of the resulting British Motor Corporation (BMC). Unfortunately the rivalry between the two companies was allowed to continue. Over time, the existence of separate sales and marketing operations along with parallel dealer networks proved counter-productive.

Before the end of the decade a new Exhibition Hall had been built, the CAB was extended and a smart new Engineering Block was completed, all reinforcing Longbridge's position as headquarters of the country's biggest car-making operation. Austin celebrated its Golden Jubilee in 1955 with grand festivities. BMC was therefore concerned when the Duke of Edinburgh appeared unimpressed by the designs he saw during a visit later that year. He reportedly criticised their lack of creativity compared with foreign competitors. Leonard Lord responded by engaging the services of Italian styling house Pininfarina. The first fruit was the Austin A40 Farina launched in 1958. Though the car's engineering was conventional, it was styled as a bright and elegant small saloon. At the same time he brought back Alec Issigonis, who had left Morris at the time of the merger. While others experimented with rear engines, gas turbines and jet age styling, Issigonis began to apply radical design concepts to the next generation of BMC cars.

The first group of true post-war designs included the A40 Devon. In the final mounting area the body was lowered onto a separate chassis frame, showing the traditional design of the car.

In 1948 Longbridge had not had time to remove the war-time camouflage. This specially designed transporter departed for the docks with four A40 saloons. Its signage proclaimed the company's pre-occupation with producing 'Austins for Dollars'.

In March 1948 the *Pacific Stronghold* was loaded with a cargo of A40s destined for the West Coast of the USA and Canada. These 420 cars represented the biggest single shipment to date and Austin exports were claimed to be earning £115 a minute for Britain.

This A40 had hit an unfortunate deer at 70mph, nineteen hours into an attempt on a twenty-four-hour endurance record. Alan Hess, Publicity Officer, organised many stunts such as this one at Long Island in 1950. Racing driver Goldie Gardner (with pipe) shared in the driving.

AUSTIN WORKERS
in the picture

Our workers this month are engaged upon the important task of packing cars for export. In this particular section cars which are completely assembled except for road wheels are enclosed in a wooden container. They are at work here on an A70 Hampshire.

EXPORT PACKING DEPARTMENT

1. J. A. Howes, Export Packer, has worked for Austins for a little over one year. Chief spare time interests are fishing and motoring; he runs an Austin 10 'Lichfield' Saloon. Married, has one child. Home, Kings Norton.

2. H. Ward, Export Packer, has been with Austins for about 22 years, including six years at the Aero factory during the war. Last two months on export packing—previously in West Works sawmill. A keen motor cyclist, also enjoys a game of darts. Married, has one child. Home, West Heath.

3. G. E. Cross, Export Packer, has recently completed two years' service with the Company. He devotes a large part of his spare time to his garden which is his chief hobby. Married, has a family of three. Home, Kings Norton.

4. J. H. Rigby, Export Packer, was with Austins as an aircraft fitter for five years before going into the Army—has been back with the Company for about 18 months. Spends a good deal of leisure time in cycling. Married, has one child. Home, Northfield.

The 'Austin Magazine' presented profiles of the four men pictured crating up an Austin A70 for export. We are told about their home life and their hobbies. Only one appears to have long service with the company, illustrating the influx of new employees after the war.

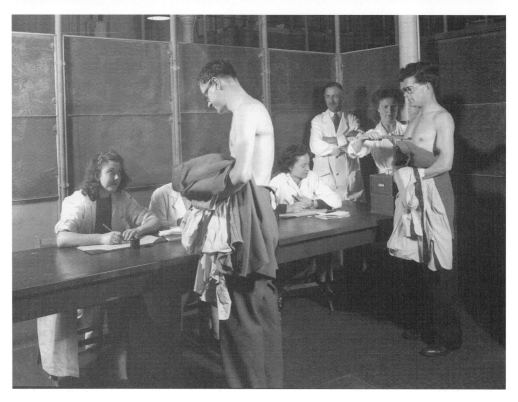

Mass radiology was offered within the factory in 1949. Behind a temporary screen well-dressed office workers removed their shirts and jackets and modestly gave their details to the efficient nurses. Some intriguing measurements were recorded.

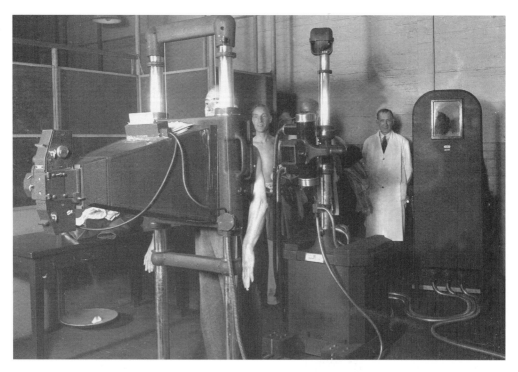

On the other side of the flimsy screens they underwent the procedure which looks rather damaging to the health of both patients and medical observers.

The stylish Austin Atlantic caught the attention of the crowd at the 1948 London Motor Show, the first to be held since the end of the war. Unfortunately it failed to do the same in the American market, for which it had been specifically designed.

The impetus to export was strong for many years. In the new CAB of 1951 an inspirational sign urged the workforce on, though they seemed more intent on completing the cars on the track. The A40 Devon sat alongside the A70 Hereford which ushered in the next style of Austin design.

Television was still a novelty, especially in Birmingham which had no transmitter until 1949. In 1950 an optimistic local shop demonstrated the 'Ekco' to a group of employees, using a blackboard and chalk to explain its mysteries. Acute eyesight was required to view the standard 9 or 12in screens.

Cars and televisions were not necessarily compatible. This A70 Hereford was being officially tested to check the engine ignition system for any signs of interference with broadcast signals. This was a common source of irritation to both viewers and listeners at the time.

An Austin subsidiary made electrically propelled vehicles, marketed from 1948 as the Morrison-Electricar. Rationing notwithstanding, the Prestwich Co-operative Society converted this 20cwt version into a well-stocked travelling grocery, butchers and fishmongers combined. Anyone for rabbit?

A taxi crosses Vauxhall Bridge with Battersea Power Station in the background. The FX3, Austin's first post-war taxi, was designed to meet the regulations governing London's 'Hackney Carriages'.

In 1950 building work began on the CAB, notable for its extensive use of glass. Its initial purpose was chassis construction. Situated on the old Flying Ground, it incorporated sixteen miles of conveyors.

The conveyor system included links to the older facilities at the bottom of the hill. This 1,000ft tunnel, 20ft below the ground, brought in painted and trimmed bodyshells as well as engines which were then combined with the chassis inside the CAB.

'Austin Magazine' labelled the CAB 'Factory of the Future in Production Today'. Its complexity required precise organisation. The marshalling stores could contain up to 750,000 chassis parts which were fed onto the tracks in unit sets.

Another important link in the communications chain was a new switchboard which was still going strong thirty years later. The supervisor enjoyed her own workstation and a padded high-backed chair, while the telephonists were provided with rather less supportive perches.

Austin made an agreement with Nissan of Japan for the A40 Somerset to be made under licence. This was initially done using the Complete Knock Down (CKD) method. Japanese workers unpacked the kits of parts which were then assembled at the Yokohama factory.

Completion of the first car was celebrated in traditional western style. Soon the Somerset would be replaced by the Cambridge. As Nissan became more experienced some elements, notably the engine, were manufactured locally.

Austin returned to the small car market in 1951 with a new Austin Seven 'A30', just before merging with Morris Motors the following year to form BMC. This was the first Austin with unitary construction (dispensing with a chassis) which fixed the name of CAB as 'Car' rather than 'Chassis' Assembly Building though previously it had been referred to by both terms. It also used the new A-series engine which was to serve the company so well.

On 9 July 1955 Longbridge celebrated its Golden Jubilee with a big party. Tickets were in great demand and the festivities included a display of historic cars and an ox roast. Lord Austin's face looked down benignly on the revellers as they got into the spirit of the event, cheering on the parade.

The Jubilee crowds were treated to all-day entertainment such as these trick cyclists. Leonard Lord, now chairman, celebrated in his own way at a family party.

An Exhibition Hall was completed ready for opening on 27 November 1956, joining the CAB and 'Kremlin' on the Flying Ground. It provided an open space 180ft long and 100ft wide, an admirable showcase for the full range of Austin and BMC products.

The same year the CAB itself was extended and the 'Flying A' Austin symbol proudly placed over one of the new entrances.

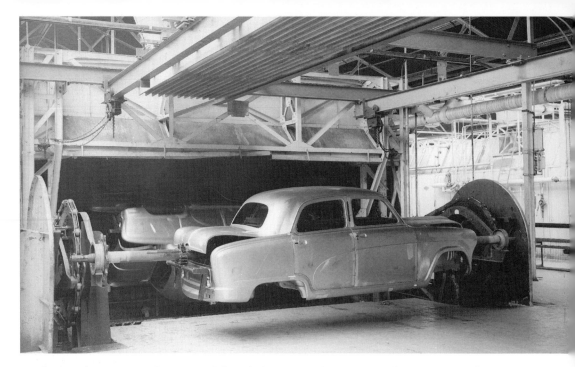

For the Rotodip process a pole was passed through the unpainted monocoque of an Austin A40, allowing it to be turned on a spit to aid de-greasing and rust-proofing. This model brought back the pre-war name of 'Cambridge'.

In 1956 a group of strikers paraded past West Works, chanting and clapping, though the ladies' sandals would suggest it was not a long march. A policeman on horseback kept a wary eye on their progress, while an enthusiastic child rode alongside on his bicycle.

During his visit to the works late in 1955 the Duke of Edinburgh was taken to see an Austin Sheerline adapted for a gas turbine 'jet' engine. The car had first become public during the Jubilee celebrations and was one of a number of such experiments in the motor industry of the time.

The Suez crisis of 1956 brought renewed oil shortages. To demonstrate its fuel efficiency an Austin A35 was sent on an economy run with an RAC observer in December. The women attend to the car while the men take a break.

In 1957 this Austin 152 van was given the striking livery of 'Surf', a best selling soap powder which made claims to 'magic power'.

The same year W.T. Hayward was pictured fixing his award from the 'Championnat National des Routiers' to his BMC diesel-engined Austin lorry. In 1961 all Austin lorry production moved, in line with government policy, to a new factory in Bathgate, Scotland.

Trying out the 1957 London Motor Show display in the factory. The pointing fingers and disembodied hands explained the 'Thirty Reasons for Austin Quality' through the various processes which went into the creation of the first generation A55.

Under the influence of American fashions, duotone paint was a popular way of cheering up the model range. Complex masking arrangements were required in the paint shop to achieve the necessary effect.

In 1954 Mr C.S. Buckley retired after thirty-nine years with the company, starting in the Road Test department and finishing as Home Sales Manager. His reward for loyal service was a modern electric fire, a set of binoculars, and a vanity set with a bunch of flowers for his wife.

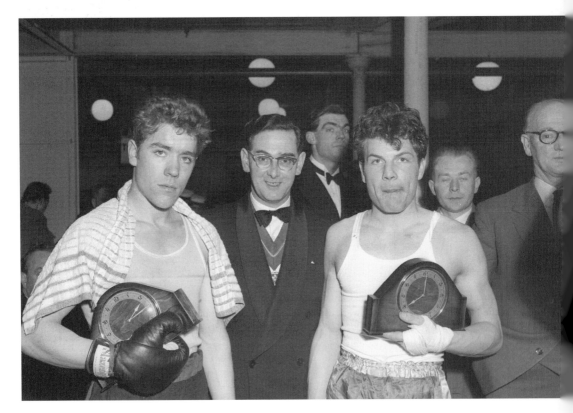

Meanwhile younger employees competed in the Works boxing tournament. The prize-winners each took home a clock to adorn their mantelpiece.

Austin set up a factory to employ disabled miners in Bargoed, Wales. It produced the 'Junior A40' pedal car, known as the J40. These expensive toys were sophisticated enough to inspire a Silverstone Junior Grand Prix. The Austin mechanic fiddled with the wiring for the electric lights and horn so the aspiring youngster in racing gear could impress the competition when finally allowed to start pedalling.

The standard of service in South Works canteen, presumably for management, was worthy of a sophisticated restaurant with its carefully laid tables and waiter/waitress service, though wine in moderation would have been wise to negotiate the zigzag pattern of the carpet afterwards.

The women in the post room preferred to dine on fish and chips with all the extras – salt and vinegar, bread and butter, fruit pies and a pot of tea.

Back at work in the large post room, parcels and letters were carefully processed, the post bag bearing the famous address 'Box 41 GPO, Birmingham'.

Leonard Lord saw computers on a visit to America and was so impressed that in 1958 he had the 'EMI CP407' installed at Longbridge to calculate the hourly paid employees pay-roll. Later a second machine was purchased for sales and production work. It also provided a safety net if the first one failed.

These were claimed to be the first electronic computers in England, using magnetic tapes and a drum for memory. In 1962 in-house newspaper 'BMC World' declared of the now five-year-old system 'BMC leads the way' showing that in its early stages computer development ran at a slower pace.

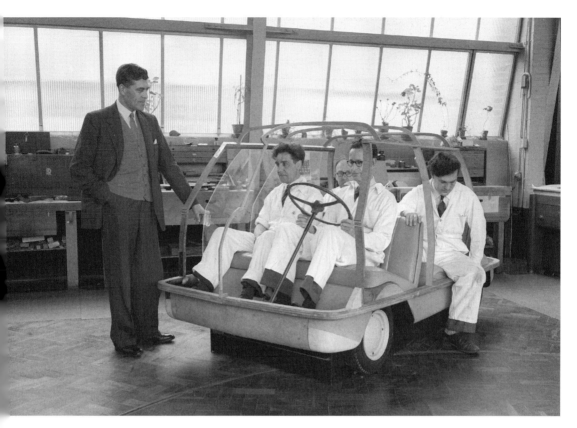

The late 1950s, just before the advent of the Issigonis Mini, was an era of experimentation for the design studio. This adventurous small car layout was designed by BMC engineer, Charles Griffin, in 1957.

Longbridge's resident Italian stylist Dick Burzi indulged in some futuristic thinking influenced by aircraft design and the shapes popular in North America.

The Italian design house of Pininfarina was engaged by Austin to produce something more saleable. Prototypes ADO 9 (Austin Drawing Office number 9) and ADO 10 were pictured in the styling studio in 1958. They became the A55 mk2 Countryman and the A99 Westminster.

The first Pininfarina design, the A40 Farina, was released that year. It was presented with and without accessories.

Six

The New Giant
1959–1975

The formation of British Leyland in 1968 created the fourth biggest motor manufacturer in the world, a formidable player in terms of jobs, finance and exports, something no government could afford to ignore.

In 1959 Longbridge was buzzing. Badge engineering was the order of the day. Different badges and minor styling differences allowed variations of the same basic design to be sold through many outlets, theoretically appealing to different types of buyers. Particular marques were no longer associated with one model or one factory. In 1959 the results of Issigonis' radical thinking were ready. In the spirit of badge-engineering his initial design was offered as an Austin Seven or a Morris Mini-Minor. These cumbersome names would soon be dropped in favour of 'Mini' a tag applied by the buying public itself. Rubber suspension, a transverse A-series engine, tiny road wheels and front wheel drive were combined into a car only 10ft long with space for four adults. Though the Mini would be produced at Longbridge for over forty years, it is largely forgotten that its big brother, the 1100, was the best seller for much of the 1960s.

Along with an expanding model range, site development continued. Storage problems were solved by the construction of a modern multi-storey car park for vehicles awaiting delivery. The space liberated was taken up by a second Car Assembly Building (CAB 2, the old building becoming CAB 1). A Design Block was added, along with a Commercial Vehicle Showroom which became known as the 'Elephant House' due to its distinctive architecture. In 1961 Leonard Lord retired and his deputy George Harriman took over. Problems were building up under the surface, but with sales booming, a leading-edge product range, home market dominance and motor sport success it is not surprising that the occupants of the 'Kremlin' failed to predict the bleak future about to engulf them.

Yet BMC was in financial trouble. In 1966 it joined with Jaguar Cars and Pressed Steel to create British Motor Holdings. Two years later, bowing to pressure from Harold Wilson's Labour Government, it merged again with the Leyland Motor Corporation (which included Standard, Triumph and Rover) to create the British Leyland Motor Corporation (which for brevity we will refer to as BL). Leyland's Chief Executive, Donald Stokes, took the role of BL Chairman showing where the balance of power lay. Longbridge became one of many factories, its Austin identity subsumed into a new Austin Morris Division. It retained the design studio, however, and thus remained a focus of future planning.

For a while BL was the fourth largest car maker in the world and dreamed great dreams. The first car from the new design team was the Morris Marina of 1971. Assembled at Cowley, the engines and gearboxes were manufactured at Longbridge. Meanwhile the 1100 design, though still a best-seller, was nearly ten years old. The Austin Allegro, developed and built at Longbridge, replaced it in 1973. On paper it improved on most of the 1100's weaknesses and offered a much wider model range. Sadly, it failed to deliver sales.

BL dominance of the home market evaporated as Ford strengthened and imports grew in volume, including the rapidly improving products of Japan. Crucially the company's image deteriorated. 'British Leyland' became a byword for rowdy strikes and poor quality products. Longbridge was closely identified with this negative image. In 1973 Edward Heath's Conservative Government faced another fuel crisis and widespread industrial unrest. Emergency restrictions were imposed on industry and the car market suddenly changed. This left the forward strategy of the Stokes team in tatters.

BMC's latest 'incredible Austin Seven' of 1959 would soon become famous as the 'Mini'. In the Exhibition Hall this theme was driven home by a magician's top hat plus a demonstration of how several adults, two dogs, a baby and the luggage seen in the foreground could all be carried in the tiny car.

Stirling Moss was lent a press fleet Austin Seven for a test drive in 1959. Unfortunately he met with an accident, inadvertently demonstrating the strength of the transverse engine to the delight of the car's designer, Alec Issigonis.

The scope of Longbridge products in 1960 was evident from the mix of vehicles awaiting despatch outside the CAB. The scene graphically illustrated the urgent need for a solution to the storage problem.

In June 1960 some new A40 Farinas and Metropolitans leaving Longbridge by train suffered a derailment right outside the factory, considerably shortening their journey.

Building a multi-storey car park in 1961 enabled the area filled with parked cars one year earlier to expand upwards, adding nine levels of extra storage. The biggest of its kind in the world, it cost £550,000 and was capable of housing 3,300 cars. It became a local landmark.

This 1961 model shows plans for the Design Block intended to concentrate BMC's creative effort in one location. The different levels of the site are evident, and the opening to a war-time tunnel under the grassy bank contrasts with the bridge linking to the 'Kremlin' above (top right).

The long running radio soap 'The Archers' is produced in Birmingham. In 1960 good publicity was to be gained by photographing agricultural story editor Godfrey Baseley and his camera-conscious dog in an appropriate setting. The Austin Gipsy was intended to rival the popular Land Rover.

In 1963 BMC were also happy to provide an A60 Countryman for recording to ensure authentic background sounds during 'Archers' episodes.

At an Austin Ex-apprentices' dinner in 1962 (an event held each December) BMC Technical Director Alec Issigonis (extreme left) enjoyed a gin and tonic with BMC Chairman George Harriman (fourth from left) and members of the committee.

Meanwhile former employees revisited the works for a party to catch up on the gossip and enjoy a sherry.

In 1963 CAB 2 was completed at a cost of £3.5 million. In the control room, a single operator had an impressive array of equipment, including three telephones, at his disposal. Longbridge's capacity was theoretically increased from 8,000 to 10,500 vehicles a week.

The 'Elephant House', seen in its original form as a commercial vehicle showroom, opened on 8 April 1965, forty years to the day before MG Rover went into administration. With its attractive architecture, its height and its prominent location it would be put to many different uses over the years.

The scale and mix of the assembly lines during the mid-1960s was breathtaking. Longbridge was at its most productive in this era. The advanced designs of Alec Issigonis – Mini, 1100 and 1800 – sat alongside the more traditional Austin products such as the A60 and A40 Farina.

In 1966 BMC and its distributors loaned 120 cars for use at the World Cup football tournament to be held in Britain that year. Some of the fleet were parked beneath the twin towers of Wembley stadium where England would take its famous victory.

BMC achieved sporting success with the Mini Cooper S, winning the prestigious Monte Carlo rally three times. Alec Issigonis, co-driver Henry Liddon, George Harriman and driver Paddy Hopkirk posed outside the Design Block with the 1964 victor, 33 EJB which, rather disappointingly, was a Morris.

Late in 1966 BMC tried to strengthen its position by merging with Jaguar and Pressed Steel to form British Motor Holdings (BMH). This cavalcade of eighty-eight vehicles outside CAB 1 demonstrated the breadth of the products and brands now in one stable.

The Austin FX4 would become the iconic London 'black cab' so beloved of foreign tourists. This one is navigating the streets of Birmingham in 1971. It was in production from 1958–97, though in later years Carbodies in Coventry had full responsibility for its manufacture.

It was not just apprentices that were nurtured for future employment. A formidable teacher presided over the school where young women destined for the office undertook training in shorthand and typing in 1961.

By 1971, computer technology was becoming less specialised. Over the next decade graduates of the typing school would become data inputters, using equipment which superseded not just the typewriter, but also numerous manual ledgers and lists. Here, clock cards were being entered onto the system.

In 1968 the Labour Government encouraged another merger, this time between the Leyland Motor Corporation and BMH. Leyland's dynamic chairman, Donald Stokes, took the same role at the new British Leyland Motor Corporation (BL), becoming its figurehead and spokesman.

A new plant was built at Cofton Hackett next to East Works to assemble the overhead camshaft E-series engine used in the Austin Maxi from 1969. Although badged an Austin, the vehicle itself was assembled at the former Morris Motors plant at Cowley.

BL suspected the advent of colour TV was affecting their sales because the price-tag was similar to the cost of trading up to a new car. Dealers Evans & Kitchen had the bright idea of linking up with Radio Rentals, ostensibly to celebrate the 1100/1300 which was still Britain's best selling car in 1971.

In 1970 trendy Birmingham pop group 'The Move' posed moodily with their new car. Oddly they had chosen the staid Vanden Plas Princess 1300, complete with walnut, leather, and picnic tables, albeit fitted with alloy wheels.

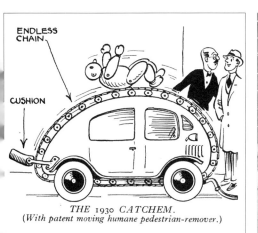

Safety was a great theme of the early 1970s. A prophetic 1930 cartoon from the 'Austin Magazine' of a 'catchem' foresaw the design of BL's Safety Research Vehicle 5 (SRV5), which echoed the joke with its nickname the 'pedestrian catcher'.

SRV5 was a modified Austin 1300 demonstrated around the Works in 1974, attracting the attention of bemused onlookers who possibly feared a fatal accident had occurred. Concern for pedestrian safety has recently re-emerged in the assessment of new designs after years of neglect.

In its earliest days BL believed it had the resources to consider a wide range of new and revised vehicles. CV154 was a large van shown in prototype form during 1971, though it was a smaller version, CV306 or the 'Sherpa' van, which went into production.

Many attempts were made to modify the Mini to make it appear more modern and improve profitability. This hatchback 'Family Mini Three-door Super' version was proposed in May 1968 though nothing like this was ever made.

The Morris Marina was the first BL-originated design and Cowley received considerable investment so production could begin in 1971. The gearbox, however, was manufactured in Longbridge's Flight Shed which was specially extended.

Longbridge investment was concentrated on the Austin Allegro. The most visible outcome was a new conveyor over the Bristol Road begun in 1971 to transport bodyshells from West Works to the facilities opposite. It became a distinctive feature of the local landscape.

A visit by Prince Philip, the Duke of Edinburgh at the end of 1972 included a trip to the 'Elephant House', which had now become a styling centre. Numerous concept drawings were pinned to the partition to give a flavour of work in progress. Donald Stokes chatted to the mayor and his party.

Meanwhile Technical Director Harry Webster proudly showed the royal visitor a mock-up of ADO 67, the Allegro, in top of the range Sport Special (SS) form. The Duke's comments on seeing the Quartic steering wheel were not recorded.

Inside CAB 1 Prince Philip inspected a more down-to-earth Mini Van. By this stage the Mini was a brand in its own right, no longer being called Austin or Morris, and all UK production had been moved to Longbridge in 1969.

An Allegro prototype was taken to the Motor Industry Research Association (MIRA) for proving. The rough pavé road thoroughly tested the interconnected fluid Hydragas system. Despite the size of the company BL did not have its own test track until the late 1970s.

The Duke of Kent came to Longbridge just before the Allegro's public announcement in May 1973. As he drove away from the Exhibition Hall, with Harry Webster in the passenger seat, BL executives anxiously awaited his verdict on 'the new driving force from Austin'.

The Allegro body was welded manually in West Works using the traditional jig frame to ensure proper alignment before it was sent on through the new conveyor. These techniques had not fundamentally changed for many years.

Early in 1975 Keith Hopkins of the Austin Morris Division posed with the model range. Longbridge manufactured engines for all these cars while Mini and Allegro were assembled there in their entirety. The centrepiece was the new 'wedge' 18/22, which would soon be renamed the Princess.

Late in 1973 poor labour relations and another oil crisis led to government-imposed energy restrictions. The Longbridge Emergency Power Control Centre was a blur of paperwork and telephones. The resulting production problems and fall in consumer demand hit BL's forward plans very hard.

FROM SKETCHBOOK TO SHOWROOM

1 The first stage in creating a new model took place in the mind of the designer. In 1945 it was possible to think about non-military vehicles for the first time since the outbreak of the Second World War. Longbridge stylist Dick Burzi happily took to his drawing board to sketch the post-war range of Austin cars.

2 A few decades later in 1970, British Leyland stylist Harris Mann used a more impressionistic style to create the eye-catching 'Diablo' concept, which would become ADO 71, the Princess.

3 In 1952, draughtsmen in the Austin drawing office turned sketches into dimensioned drawings for GS5, the Austin Cambridge. Behind them a scale model is under construction to judge the appearance of the design.

4 In front of a full-size Cambridge, Dick Burzi and Kay Petre discuss interior furnishing. Women drivers were perceived as an important market in their own right, as well as an influence on their husband's choices. So Miss Petre – a successful racing driver who had been part of the Austin Works team during the 1930s – was hired as a colour consultant by the Austin Motor Company.

5 The next step was to create a mock-up. In 1975 a team of modellers worked to translate the design sketches for ADO 88, intended as a new small car to replace the Mini, into a full-size model in wood and clay.

6 While the stylists carefully crafted the lines of the car, engineers put together a rather more crude working prototype for testing. The 'splash test' helped them determine the effectiveness of specially designed sills in diverting water away from the bodyshell. ADO 88 was rejected for reasons of style rather than any engineering shortcomings. LC8, which became the Austin Metro, took its place.

7 Once a prototype was approved it was time for manufacture to begin. Longbridge had always done much more than just assemble a final product. Parts had been forged from cast iron in the foundry since 1906. This picture was taken in 1987 shortly before this, the oldest part of the factory, was finally closed.

8 1950s: The complex process of assembling engines was carried out in the workshops of East Works, which was the new name for the wartime shadow Aero factory.

9 1950s: Over in South Works, sewing machinists undertook another skilled operation, creating the interior upholstery that would 'finish' the car.

10 The CAB 1 assembly line early in 1959, just before the advent of the revolutionary Mini. Everyday vehicles such as the Austin A35 van in the centre of the picture share the tracks with a rather more exciting two-tone Metropolitan convertible, as well as the latest A40 and A55 'Farina' designs.

11 1968: Preparation of Wolseley 18/85 bodies in West Works.

12 In 1980, 'New' West Works was opened where the manufacturing process known as 'Body in White' was heavily automated. The orange robots (left) are a blur as they weld together the bare metal bodyshells of the Rover 200 (R3), *c.* 1998.

13 In 1989 (below) the beams of the automatix laser station create a colourful light show on the bodyshell of an earlier version of the Rover 200 (R8) to check the accuracy of assembly.

14 Finally, it was time to make a sale. In 1955 glamour was used in the showroom of a small dealership to enhance the appeal of this duotone Austin A90 Six Westminster.

15 The Austin Allegro took centre stage at a rather more high-profile event, the London Motor Show held at Earl Court in 1973. British Leyland presented its latest model on a rotating dais with the slogan 'the new driving force'. The doors of this 1750 Sport version have been removed to reveal the famous 'Quartic' steering wheel.

Seven

A British Car to Beat the World

1975–1994

The Austin Metro was the first result of the search for new models to re-establish BL in the market. It was introduced with much hullabaloo in 1980 as the 'British Car to Beat the World'.

HALF THE ROBOTS IN BRITAIN CAN'T BE WRONG.

The new Metro is made at the new West Works, Longbridge, by over half the automotive welding robots in the UK.

Such precision of manufacture is backed up by individual quality control inspection.

To inspect the quality of the new 83MPG,* 12,000 miles-between-services Metro for yourself, call us for a test drive now.

It could be your finest hour.

AUSTIN
METRO
A BRITISH CAR TO BEAT THE WORLD.

When BL ran out of credit, Harold Wilson's Labour Government assumed control by taking a majority shareholding in 1975. By then, the Allegro and resilient Mini represented Longbridge's entire product range, propped up by extensive warranty schemes and price offers. It was also the centre of engine manufacture for the volume cars which meant that any problems with supply or industrial unrest affected the whole group. Effort was concentrated on a new small car. At first a direct Mini replacement was planned but the competition had moved on to hatchback 'superminis'. A change of direction was imperative. While Longbridge waited for the new model, the number of cars produced was reducing year on year. CKD kits were even being sent to BL's Belgian factory at Seneffe for assembly to be reimported to Britain for sale.

Michael Edwardes was recruited as BL's new chairman in 1977. He took a hard line both with the government and a rebellious workforce, finally breaking the cycle of industrial unrest and the drought of fresh designs. The Austin Metro was launched in October 1980, significant not just as the first new model to come out of Longbridge for seven years, but also for the modern robot technology which had been installed to produce it. For a time it was a trendy best seller, even Lady Diana Spencer drove a Metro during her courtship by Prince Charles.

Despite this progress, what BL really needed was a partner. After exploring several possibilities, a collaborative deal was forged with Honda of Japan, who had relatively little experience in car making. The first joint product was the Cowley-built Triumph Acclaim. The second was the Rover 200 built at Longbridge from 1984. Significantly Honda's version (the Ballade) was also built at Longbridge though the cars were then sent to Honda's Swindon premises to be checked over.

The 200 was internally known as the Triumph Acclaim facelift but at the last minute it was decided to use the Rover badge. Rover and MG were finally settled on as the credible brands in a quest to restore the company's tarnished image. Morris-badged cars and vans ceased in 1984, Triumph disappeared in the same year with the Acclaim. The company changed its name to Rover Group in 1986, officially banishing the last vestiges of 'British Leyland', though it would prove more difficult than this to wipe these words from the British consciousness. Austin, the marque proudly associated with Longbridge since its inception, died quietly during 1987, completing the process.

Margaret Thatcher, the Conservative Prime Minister elected in 1979, would certainly not be fooled by a change of name. Her government grudgingly allowed the development of the lightweight aluminium K-series engine to proceed together with a new gearbox design, both a vital part of future strategy. Nevertheless in 1988 she sold the government's unwanted shareholding in Rover Group to British Aerospace. All the same, the Honda collaboration seemed to have done the trick. In 1989 a new Rover 200 was launched at the British Motor Show, the first model powered by the K-series engine (though a Honda engine was an option). The success enjoyed by this car along with the '400' saloon version was very welcome. For a brief period in the early 1990s the popularity of the family-sized cars coming out of Longbridge seemed to offer hope that its fortunes could be revived.

A Wolseley version of the 1100 was introduced in 1965. This decorative display was precisely parked outside the glass frontage of CAB 1 in readiness for a dealer drive-away. In the background the Exhibition Hall still carried the 'Austin of England' logo.

By 1977 the same area was looking distinctly run down when BL embarked on a rebuilding programme to create an up-to-date assembly area for their much-heralded small car. Instead of neat lines of Wolseleys there are just a few scattered Minis.

In July 1978, the side of CAB 1 was being extended, the glass framework disappearing inside. A new exterior was constructed, in brick (as here) or metal. The result, while less distinctive, provided a more worker-friendly environment. Allegro bodyshells were being stored outside CAB 2 opposite.

Later that year a major fire blazed in some of the wartime tunnels, now mostly used as storage. One casualty was this Vanden Plas prototype. The Design Block overhead also had a narrow escape as worried staff found the floor becoming alarmingly warm.

The ultra-modern Metro body plant was finished with the same style of cladding as CAB 1. Known as 'new West Works' from the air, it dominated its surroundings. From the road, however, it was hidden behind the red brick frontage of 'old West Works', now one of the oldest areas of the site.

On 22 October 1980, shortly after the Metro launch, Prince Charles came to tour the new plant and officially open the new West Works. Chairman Michael Edwardes and Managing Director Harold Musgrove watched attentively as he signed the visitor's book.

New West Works was a high, steel-framed building offering a vast uninterrupted space perfect for the level of automated assembly which would characterise the Metro. Robots welded together panels to create bodyshells which moved from station to station on programmed conveyors.

The Sciaky automated body framing line marked the point where the underfloor, monosides, roof and front end came together to create a complete bodyshell. It offers a stark contrast to previous scenes of busy people welding by hand on cluttered tracks.

Mrs Thatcher, recently elected Conservative Prime Minister, agreed to appear on stage with the Metro when it was publicly announced. But she was not keen to provide open-ended support for BL. In 1988 her government returned the company to private ownership by selling it to British Aerospace.

THIS COULD BE YOUR FINEST HOUR.

WE'LL HIT THEM WITH PRESS ADS.   **WE'LL CLOBBER THEM WITH POSTERS.**   **WE'LL BEAT THEM WITH TELEVISION.**

METRO ARRIVES OCTOBER 14

It was vital to BL that the Metro should succeed. This inspired a massive promotional effort with a strongly patriotic theme. To the backdrop of a carefully orchestrated media campaign, dealers teased the public by hiding the long-awaited car under Union flags, to be revealed on launch day.

Inside CAB 1, the Metro body was united with the rest of car by being lowered onto its mechanical parts. These included the Hydragas suspension spheres and a specially revised A-series engine. Seeing the car laid out in this way illustrates the compactness of the design.

In an attempt to counter their reputation for poor quality, BL built a Customer Validation Building (CVB) where finished cars were fettled and checked after leaving the revamped CAB 1. Here a Metro 'L' had its distinguishing go-faster stripe added.

Michael Edwardes planned a 'product led revival'. Styling bucks for the Montego project were made in the Longbridge styling studio. Along with its smaller brother, the Maestro, it would be assembled at Cowley though both were badged as Austins.

To make way for Montego and Maestro, the line for the old Marina (now renamed Ital) had to be moved. The first Longbridge-built versions were completed in September 1982. They would be the last vehicles to carry the Morris badge. This meant 'Morris' came to an end in the traditional home of Austin.

By 1983 drawing boards were being replaced by computer terminals as 'Computer Aided Design' (CAD) became the norm. BL was at the forefront of its development.

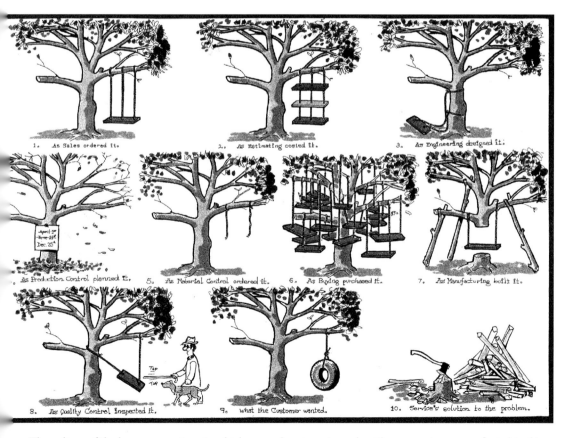

The culture of the large corporation, in which many departments speak with many voices, was reflected in this cartoon on the theme of quality which dates from June 1987.

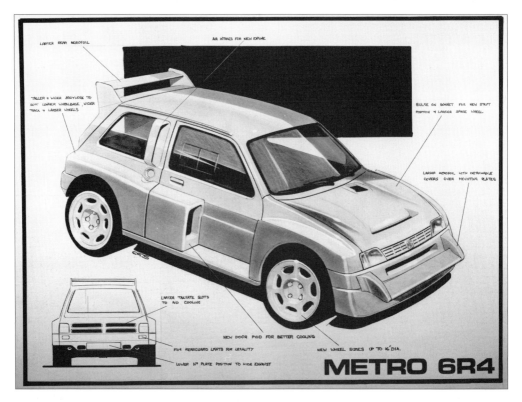

The fastest small car from Longbridge? The MG badge had been successfully applied to the Metro since 1982. The MG Metro 6R4 was the ultimate rally version, intended to compete under regulations that unfortunately changed before it could show its merit.

It took forty years for Longbridge to make one million cars. Almost forty years on, in 1985, the ten millionth was celebrated exuberantly with dancing girls, to the apparent delight of some of the workforce.

After rumours of link-ups with Renault and Chrysler UK, BL finally signed a collaborative deal with Honda of Japan on 15 May 1979. At the press conference, Sir Michael Edwardes and Mr Kawashima shook on the deal.

Honda's Ballade, pictured in their styling studio, was modified to become the Rover 200 in 1984. Not only was it the first Japanese design to be built at Longbridge, it was also the first 'Rover' to emerge from the factory.

The lonely life of preparing wheels and tyres for fitment with only a corporate notice for company. The overhead track being stocked feeds into the assembly line shown in the picture below.

Japanese production techniques were introduced into CAB 2. On the Rover 200 final assembly track cars were suspended on cradles as they moved between stations rather than proceeding along the floor on mobile trestles.

Another innovation was the 'stuff up' method whereby components were elevated into the car rather then the car being lowered down onto them as we saw with the Metro earlier. Here an engine was being fitted.

The employee manning the desk inside the quiet of the Exhibition Hall reception in 1987 seemed to have chosen the telephone rather than the bust of Herbert Austin (extreme right) for conversation.

Rather more down to earth was the personnel foyer in the old office block by K Gate. A young receptionist with an impressive hairstyle imparted some information, possibly, as the notice on the desk indicated, that there were 'no application forms available'.

In 1982 the Exhibition Hall dining room 'self service' area received extensive upgrading. A professional chef prepared an appetising display of meat and vegetables ready for lunch.

In 1987 the factory photographer, John Chasemore, was given the task of recording some of the other facilities. This set of pictures was labelled 'poor rest areas' – quite!

Total Quality Improvement (TQI) was a business technique becoming widespread in industry by 1990. This small group were being invited to give their opinion on the virtues and faults of the Metro.

At ten years old the Metro received a new engine, gearbox and revised suspension. The advertising campaign stressed its engineering but underplayed its acquisition of a Rover badge.

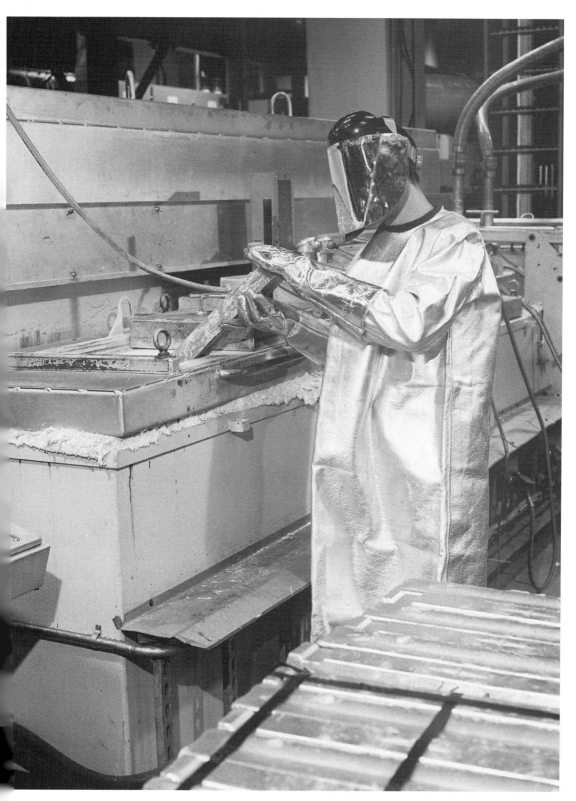

Major investment resulted in the technologically advanced K–series engine in 1989. This space-age operator was processing bars of aluminium, the metal which contributed to its efficiency. He was provided with considerably more protection than his counterpart in the old foundry. The Low Pressure Sandcasting facility was developed in East Works at a cost of £12 million.

The K-series engine design won the Queen's Award for Technology in 1992. The trophy was proudly displayed by Paul Kirk, Managing Director of Power Train, the engine and gearbox division which was now based in East Works.

Consumer clinics had become an important part of car development and marketing. Here two Rovers were compared to market rivals from BMW and Volvo by a selected sample of potential customers.

The next Rover 200 was based on the Honda Concerto. From 1989 both were built at Longbridge. Here we see the automatic fitting of a windscreen to a Honda version in CAB 1.

Using a technique introduced by Honda, doors were assembled separately from the car to allow better access and avoid damage. Here a Rover 216 receives back its completed doors at the end of the build programme.

During 1990 Mini sales were reinvigorated by the revival of Cooper versions. A delighted John Cooper visited the factory to give his approval to the initiative.

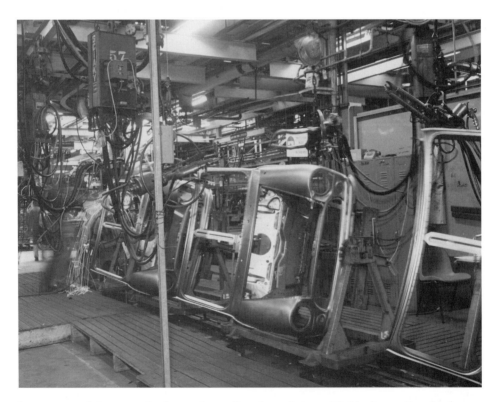

In contrast to all the new technology and manufacturing techniques, Mini bodies continued to be produced using time-honoured methods in a part of old West Works dating from the First World War.

'80 years of Austin' was officially celebrated in 1986, including a dinner on 26 April to echo the 1906 event. Harold Musgrove played his part by posing with a Class 47 Locomotive, number 47337, named 'Herbert Austin'. The Austin badge and name, however, were quietly dropped during 1987.

It was therefore ironic that when Rover Group added a 'retro' grille to the Rover 200 in 1993, they chose an Austin Somerset rather than a classic Rover to appeal to the nostalgia of their audience, using the slogan 'forty years of chrome grilles'.

When Honda expanded their Swindon facility they no longer needed Longbridge to build their cars. The last Concerto was bid farewell with due ceremony. Honda and Rover workers were each dressed in their own 'corporate workwear', a Japanese concept intended to overcome status barriers in the workplace.

By 1993 the Rover Group range covered much of the marketplace. The smaller six cars on the left were Longbridge-built, the rest from Cowley. The benefits of collaboration and new engines were reaping rewards. The British Aerospace era, however, was drawing to a close.

Eight

The End of the Road
1994–2005

In its heyday, Longbridge had been the headquarters of a massive corporation, manufacturing a plethora of brands and models for worldwide export. The failure of British Leyland's model strategy meant that by 1990 the company was preoccupied with reversing its decline in the marketplace. Collaboration with Honda contributed to a new range of well-engineered products, but the decision made by British Aerospace in 1994 to sell the company on to the German luxury car-maker BMW AG prompted Honda to withdraw. Sadly, BMW's efforts to use the Rover brand to translate itself from a premium manufacturer to a mainstream producer were not to be successful, spelling the end of mass production on the Longbridge site.

Chief Executives Berndt Pischetsrieder (BMW) and John Towers (Rover Group) pose with an MG RV8 shortly after the takeover.

It was no surprise when British Aerospace sold Rover Group at the earliest opportunity in 1994, but the bidder's identity, Bavarian car-maker BMW, was less expected.

Initially, the local management remained in charge, though Chief Executive John Towers left in 1996. Things started well, with three new products already waiting for launch. Hopes for the future, however, rested on development of the Rover 75, BMW's interpretation of a luxury Rover. The car was to be produced at Cowley, which had been extensively redeveloped by British Aerospace. It was launched at the 1998 Motor Show in Birmingham, but BMW was disappointed when initial sales figures did not match their expectations.

The parent company began to take a more active role in Rover Group's management and continued with plans for a small car code-named R50, which was to be launched using the 'Mini' name. It was partly designed at Longbridge, and the Birmingham factory was undergoing extensive redevelopment to accommodate the new manufacturing facilities needed to produce it.

It therefore came as a shock when BMW announced its intention to sell Rover Group in March 2000. The R50 would be transferred to the Cowley plant, which was to be retained. The valuable Land Rover marque was sold to Ford, a deal that included the Solihull factory and the Gaydon Test Centre. But initially the only offers made for Longbridge came from venture capitalists, who proposed a switch to niche products with the loss of many jobs.

In May, local opinion, media pressure and Tony Blair's Labour government all influenced BMW's decision to sell the Longbridge Works to the Phoenix consortium for a nominal £10. The consortium was led by John Towers, along with three other businessmen who all had associations with pre-BMW Rover Group. They pledged to maintain volume car production, adopting the name 'MG Rover Group' for the new enterprise, though within a few years the workforce had been cut back from around 12,000 to 6,000. To compensate for the loss of the promised small car, BMW allowed the new company to replace R50 with the Rover 75.

Longbridge was the oldest working car factory in Britain and still one of the largest. The strong MG brand was applied to existing models with great success. To secure a long-term future, however, what was really needed was a model of medium size and price to replace the Honda-based Rover 45. Lacking capital of their own, MG Rover looked for a collaborator – a search that would dominate the next few years. Proton of Malaysia and China Brilliance were both pursued. A deal was struck with TATA of India to revamp the Indica hatchback into the CityRover. This was imported and offered at optimistic prices with woeful lack of success. In the meantime, to provide cash, key assets were sold including the land and buildings, which were then leased back from development company St Modwen Properties.

In 2003 fresh talks began with the Shanghai Automotive Industry Corporation (SAIC) but after two years negotiations failed, precipitating the crisis that sent MG Rover into administration on 8 April 2005. Throughout the summer of 2005 the administrators kept the site ticking over while they sought a buyer. On 22 July, it was announced that the remaining assets of the company (including the Austin marque) had been sold to the Nanjing Automobile Corporation (NAC), a Chinese company looking to expand into Europe.

By 1994, the 'portfolio' project was already under way on a tight budget and three models arrived in rapid succession just after the BMW takeover. The Rover 400 was based on a Honda Civic; the Rover 200 and MGF came from largely independent thinking. They are pictured in front of the 'Kremlin'.

Longbridge underwent some further development during the 1990s. Number 3 Paint Plant incorporated a sophisticated computer control room whose window looked over the new facility.

The Education Partnership organised visits from local schools. The MGF sportscar was shown to a group of children dressed in rather outsized workwear, which was now theoretically standard uniform throughout the factory. Their grey coats, which usually carried the worker's name, were instead labelled 'young engineer'.

The canteens were not the only source of food. This picture was taken in 1996 to mark the retirement of Maisie, driver of one of the chuckwagons, which were a familiar sight around the plant.

The last Rover 100 (the renamed Metro) was built on 23 December 1997. A volume small car had been the mainstay of Longbridge production for much of its history. This would become the last, though limited Mini production continued for another three years.

The K-series engine underwent major development. A V6 version in 1996 enabled Rover to dispense with Honda engines in its large cars. These two engineers had their workstation at a desk situated outside the hot test booth in Power Train.

Site development included plans for new production facilities for a small car to be assembled at Longbridge. This involved demolishing an area of derelict buildings in South Works, including the disused foundry which had closed in 1987.

Our old friend and reference point, the water tower, was the oldest landmark surviving from the original White & Pike factory. It was in such a perilous state by late 1998 that it too had to be demolished.

The model behind all this activity was R50, to be marketed as MINI. In 1999 Herr Schulze, Head of Plant Munich, visited Longbridge, where part of its development was taking place. The door mirror of this prototype seemed to be causing some concern.

Early in 2000, BMW invited the Longbridge workforce to the Exhibition Hall to present plans for their future within BMW Group. The newly facelifted Rover 25 and 45 models were the centrepiece of the display.

At the same event, employees and their families were able to walk round a large model of the proposed changes to the factory. CAB 2 had already been extensively redeveloped. The display panels on the wall

identified Cowley (Plant Oxford) as the site of large car manufacturing. Longbridge (Plant Birmingham) would produce the smaller Rover models while becoming 'Home of the Mini'. Within two months, BMW had gone.

BMW's decision was so sudden that it was inevitably followed by weeks of uncertainty, causing much worry and concern throughout Rover Group's workforce. Longbridge's fate was the last to be decided but, after considerable pressure from the local community, trade unions and the British government, it was decided to sell the factory for a nominal £10 to the Phoenix consortium, which would become better known as 'the Phoenix Four'. This picture shows three of them, (right to left) John Towers, Peter Beale and Nick Stephenson, holding a framed copy of the bank note and standing beside an MGF. The absent director was John Edwards.

MG Rover's Longbridge manufacturing site covers an area of land stretching to over 400 acres. Both physically and emotionally it can claim to be the true heart of Britain's motor industry. A workforce of 5,500 highly-skilled men and women help to assemble the current MG Rover range, many of them following in their parents' footsteps onto assembly lines and into paintshops.

This rich motor-manufacturing heritage is an enormously valuable skills base which will allow MG Rover and its customers to take maximum advantage of this single-site manufacturing resource. A supply chain employing 27,000 people delivers high-quality components from the immediate West Midlands area, while many more companies contribute their skills from further afield. In fact Rover cars require the combined capabilities of over 500 suppliers worldwide, involving an annual spend on production material of £12bn. By value, 80% of this impressive figure is spent with UK based companies, 15% with companies in mainland Europe while the remaining 5% of components are sourced from around the world. Currently, four models are produced at Longbridge, but this will soon increase to an eight-model line up. We're particularly proud of the smooth inception, on time and on budget, of the Rover 75 production line following a £35m civil engineering investment programme.

The new owners issued a brochure emphasising the skills and commitment of the workforce. On the first anniversary of their purchase of Longbridge they gave each employee a card of thanks with £10 cash enclosed.

At the end of 2000, Managing Director Kevin Howe welcomed the Duke of Edinburgh to CAB 1. An inspirational banner hung over the rolling road test area as the company's plans were outlined to him.

As part of the deal the traditional Mini had to make way for BMW's new small car. On 4 October 2000, a press day was held to mark the last Mini off the production line. Lulu emerged from the car under the glare of lights and to the applause of the workforce. Meanwhile, the first Longbridge-built Rover 75 sat alongside attracting rather less razzmatazz, even though it would be crucial to the success or failure of an independent Longbridge.

Two months earlier, in August, the A-series engine had been discontinued after nearly fifty years of powering a succession of popular cars. The Mini was the last car still using Longbridge's longest serving power unit, so this marked the end for them both.

The multi-storey car park had become a safety hazard as well as a landmark. It was demolished in August 2001, radically changing the appearance of the factory's main entrance at Q Gate. Ironically the area liberated reverted to a ground-level car park for vehicles awaiting despatch.

Teardown of a different kind. In an effort to reduce manufacturing costs, the components of each car and the way they were assembled were carefully examined for any potential savings.

A great asset to the new company was the ownership of the MG marque, which was applied successfully across the Rover range. In 2001 the 'Le Mans Powergirls' posed with an MG ZR (based on the Rover 25). It carried the X-Power branding which was devised to reinforce the sporting badge.

At the Maxpower Live show in 2004, an MG ZS (Rover 45) was fitted with an interactive video screen in the hope of attracting the youth market, though this potential customer seems too young to have a driving licence.

The Rover 75 nevertheless continued to be the key product as the rest of the model range began to age. At the Birmingham Motor Show in 2004, Gordon Brown (then Chancellor of the Exchequer) was shown the latest version by James Turnbull, John Millett, Rob Oldaker and Toni Oakley.

The Elephant House became a visitor centre encompassing a showpiece sales area. Shortly afterwards MG Rover Direct was set up to sell used cars. Many enthusiasts made a special journey for the privilege of buying from the factory.

In order to fund the new models that were badly needed, the search for business partners carried on. In December 2002, John Towers signed the paperwork to conclude a deal with TATA, using a video link to India set up in the visitor centre.

VISIONARY

The Rover Tourer Concept Vehicle (TCV) is an exciting glimpse into the innovative design you can expect from Rover's next generation of cars. It combines unparalleled levels of versatility and functionality in a stylish and dynamically accomplished five seater. With a powerful stance, high ground clearance and a distinctive look, it projects a bold new personality for Rover. Active families will love the TCV's highly adaptable interior and clever load carrying configurations, while business people will appreciate its comprehensive 'work-on-the-move' capability.

The Tourer Concept Vehicle (TCV), styled by MG Rover designer Peter Stevens, embodied the aspiration for a mid-sized Rover. Publicity material stressed the functionality and adaptability of the proposal.

A mildly revised version of the TATA Indica, a small Indian hatchback, was all that could actually be delivered. The original concept from October 2002 displayed function rather than style, though crude wheel covers were added to imitate alloys. It was imported and sold as the CityRover.

The MG SV was one of the most expensive vehicles ever to come out of Longbridge. Manufactured in Italy and finished at Longbridge, it was derived from a De Tomaso design. Unfortunately, what MG Rover needed was a new medium-sized car for the volume market, not an exotic supercar.

China seemed the best hope for an overseas investor. Throughout 2004 representatives of the Shanghai Automotive Industry Corporation (SAIC) visited Longbridge as part of ongoing negotiations. In April 2005, talks collapsed and car production was abruptly halted as the company plunged into administration.

The notice advising caution against moving vehicles which hung over CAB 1's rolling road area was unnecessary in the first few days after administration began. As the assembly hall ground to a halt, those cars that were complete enough had been put through the testing booths and the normal bustle ceased.

Soon, however, activity resumed. Chronic supply problems meant that a number of vehicles around the site were awaiting vital components. Once parts had been obtained, cars such as these 25/45 models and their MG derivatives were brought back into CAB 1 to undergo the testing required to release them.

There was also a series of vehicles that were not yet built but had progressed far enough through the system to be completed. This Rover 75 would be the last vehicle to make its way through the assembly hall. In normal circumstances it would take four hours to reach the test booths at the end of the line. In this case it required almost three months of hand building because large sections of the automated system

could not be used for such a small volume of cars. The windscreen was fitted manually, just in front of the robot glazing cell behind the 'KEEP OUT' sign. Due to continuing parts shortages, it lacked the bumper covers and headlights normally fitted by this stage, which provided an opportunity for the remaining workers to add their signatures to the impact bar above the words 'LAST ONE ON LINE'.

Long-planned celebrations for the Austin Centenary weekend went ahead in Cofton Park in July 2005. Blessed with fine weather, enthusiasts were determined that the events across the road would not divert them from a shared enjoyment of Longbridge's proud heritage of vehicles.

After protracted negotiations with several parties, including SAIC, in August 2005 the administrators signed a surprise deal with the Nanjing Automobile Corporation (NAC) for the purchase of MG Rover's remaining assets, including the MG, Austin and Morris marques.

Nine

Longbridge Future

The Conference Centre had taken on many identities since it was built in the Jubilee year of 1955. It is pictured here in May 2005 through the doors of CAB 1, shortly after MG Rover went into administration. Difficult as this period was for the local community, after a necessary period of demolition the focus would shift to reconstruction and the creation of a new infrastructure of offices, houses and shops.

The sudden collapse of MG Rover occurred just short of 100 years after Herbert Austin set up business at Longbridge. Austin himself had a close brush with financial disaster in 1921, but the firm pulled through that and many other difficulties throughout the years. This time, however, there was no solution to be found. There was an emotional as well as a financial impact, not just on the workforce, dealerships and suppliers, but on the wider local community whose lives had been dominated by the industrial giant in their midst for so many years. The next decade would demonstrate the resilience of the people of Longbridge, and their determination to pull together in changing circumstances.

There was naturally a strong desire to see the motor industry continue to have a presence locally. The Nanjing Automobile Corporation (NAC) retained a base at Longbridge, establishing a research and development operation on an area of the site leased from St Modwen Properties. Much of the tooling and machinery was shipped to a new factory in Nanjing where a series of MG-badged cars based on the 2005 Longbridge product range went into production.

There was a complication, however, as the Shanghai Automotive Industry Corporation (SAIC), which had been negotiating with MG Rover prior to the collapse, had already bought the intellectual rights to these same models. They began to manufacture an alternative product under the badge 'Roewe' in their own factory in Shanghai. In 2007, the Chinese government stepped in to encourage the rivals to join together and SAIC finally took control of the MG brand along with the Longbridge factory. The British operation was renamed 'MG Motor UK' and significant investment was put into a design centre in the old sales and marketing block where work began on a new model range. CAB 1, meanwhile, assembled cars from parts manufactured in and imported from China.

It was recognised, however, that Longbridge's days as the hub of British motor manufacture were over and that economic diversification would be essential to the regeneration of the area. St Modwen had acquired the first plot of land from MG Rover in 2001, and had taken on the whole site by 2004. As MG Rover's business shrank, plans were made to redevelop some of the more derelict areas of the vast factory site. The collapse precipitated a complete revision of existing proposals, which now had to encompass the much bigger footprint of West Works, North Works, South Works, East Works and Flight Shed.

Inevitably, the first few years were dominated by demolition of long-neglected factory buildings, followed by the need to cleanse ground that had been subject to so many years of industrial activity, to make it suitable for other types of use. But by 2010 a new town centre was taking shape. Among the newcomers attracted to the area were the further education institution Bournville College, business enterprises such as Sainsbury's and Marks & Spencer's, extensive housing estates and a retirement village. The history of the site was not forgotten. The focus of the new town centre was 'Austin Park' whose pathways featured a historical timeline. Streets and buildings were given names to echo the past – Devon Way, East Works Drive, Seven House and the Cambridge pub to name a few. In addition, signs were erected in front of new landmark buildings expressing the sentiments of local residents about both the past and the future.

I SLEPT TO THE SOUND OF THE HAMMERS

Since 1973, the conveyor across the Bristol Road had stood as a landmark to travellers heading out of Birmingham, marking their arrival at the boundary of a major car factory. Its removal would be the first intensive engineering challenge for St Modwen, which hired one of the largest cranes in the country to carefully dismantle the heavy concrete structure piece by piece over the weekend of 5–6 August 2006.

It was a delicate operation close to a densely populated area, adjacent to a major A road and over a railway bridge. It therefore required great patience and skill to complete the task safely. At the end of a hot summer day, the crane crew deservedly celebrated their achievement when all was successfully concluded.

Old West Works had been little used for many years and the buildings were in poor repair. They were therefore the first to be demolished during 2006 (above and below) exposing the interior of the old factory, including some of the original toilet blocks beneath the characteristic zig-zag roofs.

K Gate (above) was the original entrance to the factory and served as the main gateway until operations shifted towards the old flying ground and Q Gate took over that function. Just inside sat the impressive South Engineering block built in 1957.

Nothing, however, was sacred. In February 2007 K Gate was dismantled, followed shortly by the demolition of the buildings around.

The wartime tunnels continued to be an unending source of fascination to many, but by 2000 they had become so unsafe that it was necessary to block the entrances to prevent curious adventurers from entering them. This was the entrance to Tunnel A, which sat next to the railway line, in 2007.

Flight shed, with its impressive roof structure, was one of the later buildings to be handed over. This picture of its distinctive single-span roof was taken shortly before demolition began in November 2011.

As St Modwen worked on the bigger plan, NAC concentrated its activities on the cluster of buildings in the vicinity of the Q Gate entrance. In early March 2007 the totem outside still carried the old MG Rover signage (left). A few weeks later it was rebranded with the NAC name and a new MG badge (right).

In 2008, following the merger with SAIC, the totem was simplified to reflect the new UK incarnation of the company (left). In February 2011 a new corporate identity was unveiled declaring that 'the bold new look captures the essence of MG as having a famous past and a really exciting future'. Accordingly the totem changed its colour from white to red, as did the signage above the gate itself (right).

Initially the new Chinese owners of the MG brand turned to the model that had been in production at the time of their takeover. The MG TF was relaunched under the slogan 'Fun is Back' and appeared at the London Motor Show in August 2008 (above) followed by the Birmingham Classic Car Show in November (below).

While St Modwen worked on cleaning the land and obtaining planning permission for longer-term development, they put up the first phase of the 'Longbridge Technology Park' during 2006–07. Called the Innovation Centre, it was intended to attract entrepreneurs such as Herbert Austin himself had once been. By 2015 it was operating at full occupancy with an impressive range of modern businesses.

Spearheading incomers would be Bournville College which was constructed on the site of North Works, forming the heart of the new town centre and signalling the fact that rebuilding was finally beginning in earnest. Pictured above in January 2011, it opened to students in the academic year of 2012. The striking structure would form a visual cue to those travelling out of Birmingham on the Bristol Road in the same way as the old conveyor had once done. The low building on the left was given a striking gold-coloured fascia, while the main college block on the right was clad in bright blue.

The Longbridge of the twenty-first century would have to be built on a far wider economic base than before to have a sustainable future, and an important part of the mix would be new housing. In 2011 St Modwen completed the first phase of an estate bounded by Lickey Road and Lowhill Lane, replacing General Office Block and the experimental department. It abutted directly on to the raised area where the Elephant House still stood and was separated from the remaining factory buildings by a line of trees. The houses proved very popular, quickly selling out.

In 2012 Persimmon Homes began work on an even bigger estate on the site of East Works, which proved equally popular, with houses being sold and occupied almost as quickly as they were completed.

The changing face of Longbridge. As factory buildings disappeared, a new town centre took their place. In the centre of this aerial shot (taken in March 2015), a new crossroads has been created on the site of North Works, a focal point for the Innovation Centre, Bournville College (with the Austin Park behind) and Sainsbury's. Further back, South Works is still under development. On the extreme right, the Bristol Road bisects the picture. West

rks has become a car park while further along is the island where K Gate used to sit. In the distance, lying within footprint of the old flying ground, is the area under lease to MG Motor UK. Though not on the scale of the inal Austin factory, its size was still substantial. Clustered around the old Q Gate, it incorporated surviving buildings as the Elephant House, the Conference Centre and CABs 1 and 2.

On the retail front, Sainsbury's led the way, opening a large store in the new town centre in August 2012. Nearby were other big names such as the Premier Inn with a Beefeater Restaurant and Costa Coffee.

Meanwhile, MG Motor UK were still handing parts of the site back to St Modwen. The Design Block was transferred in August 2012. The main building, where Alec Issigonis had once had an office, was quickly demolished, leaving the old bridge from the Kremlin (which was still part of the area occupied by MG) straddling the boundary fence where it linked to a stranded doorway.

Work in progress. In February 2015, locals take a stroll through Austin Park. In the background construction continues on a new Marks and Spencer's superstore alongside a car park and several smaller units.

Meanwhile MG Motor UK continued to go out and about to promote its new models. In the foreground is the medium-sized MG 6, with the smaller MG 3 hatchback behind.

The Longbridge Public Art Project was established to promote cultural life as part of regeneration. In October 2014, the Longbridge Light Festival attracted huge crowds to the new town centre. Its theme, 'Back to the Future', aimed to celebrate the past while looking forward with optimism to what the future might bring.

Alongside the work of professional artists, the local community was eager to be involved with the event. The enthusiastic pupils of Turves Green Girls' School put on an impressive lantern parade.

This portrait of Herbert Austin was painted by the American cartoonist 'Sphinx' in 1907, not long after Austin had set up a business in his own name for the first time. He was 40 years old and would go on to build the Austin Motor Company into a major enterprise, transforming a rural outpost of Birmingham into an economic powerhouse. Though car manufacture no longer dominates the area, it has left an indelible mark on the landscape, culture and heritage of Longbridge.

If you enjoyed this book, you may also be interested in...

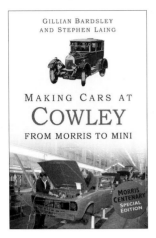

Making Cars at Cowley: From Morris to MINI

GILLIAN BARDSLEY & STEPHEN LAING

978 0 7524 9146 2

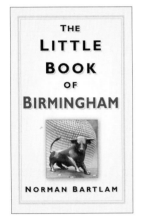

The Little Book of Birmingham

NORMAN BARTLAM

978 0 7524 6349 0

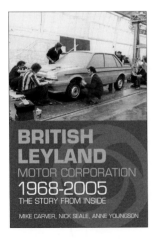

British Leyland Motor Corporation 1968–2005: The Story from Inside

MIKE CARTER, NICK SEALE & ANNE YOUNGSON

978 0 7509 6144 8

Visit our website and discover thousands of other History Press books.

www.thehistorypress.co.uk